INDEPENDENT ACADEMIC RESEARCH STUDIES

ABUSED NO MORE
VOICES OF REFUGEE
ASYLUM-SEEKING WOMEN

Holly Challenger

Independent Academic Research Studies (IARS)
With funding from Comic Relief and Matrix Chambers

Independent Academic Research Studies (IARS)
IARS PUBLICATIONS
159 Clapham Road, London SW9 0PU, United Kingdom
+44(0) 20 7820 0945 contact@iars.org.uk www.iars.org.uk

IARS is a leading, international think-tank with a charitable mission to give everyone a chance to forge a safer, fairer and more inclusive society. IARS achieves its mission by producing evidence-based solutions to current social problems, sharing best practice and by supporting young people to shape decision making. IARS is an international expert in restorative justice, human rights and inclusion, citizenship and user-led research.

IARS' vision is a society where everyone is given a choice to actively participate in social problem solving. The organisation is known for its robust, independent evidence-based approach to solving current social problems, and is considered to be a pioneer in user-involvement and the application of user-led research methods.

Published in the UK by IARS Publications
© 2013 IARS
The moral rights of the author have been asserted
Database right IARS Publications (maker)
First published May 2013

All rights reserved. No part of this publication may be reproduced, stored in a retrieval system or transmitted, in any form or by any means, without the prior permission in writing of IARS Publications, or as expressly permitted by law, or under terms agreed with the appropriate reprographics rights organisation. Enquiries concerning reproduction outside of the scope of the above should be sent to IARS at the address above.
You must not circulate this book in any other binding or cover and you must impose the same condition on any acquirer.

British Library Cataloguing in Publication Data
Layout: dennis@kavitagraphics. Printed in the UK by The Russell Press

ISBN 978-1-907641-23-7

INDEPENDENT ACADEMIC RESEARCH STUDIES

Table of Contents

Preface & Acknowledgements: Dr Theo Gavrielides,   01
Founder & Director of IARS
Foreward: Lynne Berry OBE, Director of Public Benefit   05

Introduction and impetus for the book   07
1.1   Introduction   07
1.2   Book structure   09

Research strategy   11
2.1   Methodology and IARS' user-led, action research ethos   11
2.2   Overview of the participants and sampling strategy   15

The impact of gender and experiences of gender-related persecution on refugee and asylum seeking women in the UK: a review of the literature   21
3.1   Refugee and asylum seeking women in the UK   21
3.2   Gender-related persecution   22
3.3   Claiming asylum   25
3.4   Refugee women's vulnerability to sexual violence   33
3.5   Accessing services and support   35
3.6   Summary of the extant literature and current knowledge   41

Refugee and asylum seeking women's experiences of health services in Greater London: Findings from the fieldwork   45
4.1   Introduction   45
4.2   Accessing health services   45
4.3   Building a relationship with one GP   50
4.4   Problems associated with language, culture and communication   53

Refugee and asylum seeking women's experiences of legal services in Greater London: Findings from the fieldwork — 57
- 5.1 Introduction — 57
- 5.2 Finding a solicitor — 57
- 5.3 Communication and cultural challenges — 62

What matters when receiving legal and health services — 67
- 6.1 Introduction — 67
- 6.2 Building trusting relationships — 67
- 6.3 Feeling listened to — 69
- 6.4 The importance of empathy — 74

Discussion & recommendations — 83
- 7.1 Introduction — 83
- 7.2 The importance of building trust and communicating empathy — 84
- 7.3 A need for more time — 85
- 7.4 The importance of the gender — 87
- 7.5 Problems with registering with GP practices — 88
- 7.6 Consistency of healthcare — 89
- 7.7 Provision of language support services in GP services — 91
- 7.8 The use of informal interpreters in GP services — 92
- 7.9 Awareness of entitlement to legal aid — 93
- 7.10 The impact of detention and dispersal on access to solicitors' services — 94
- 7.11 A shortage of legal aid solicitors — 95
- 7.12 A need for better correspondence with solicitors — 96
- 7.13 The presence of children in solicitor appointments — 97

Bibliography — 99

- Appendix A: About IARS — 109
- Appendix B: About the author and research team — 110

Tables & Figures

Figure 1: Immigration status and number of research participants   15
Figure 2: Participants' Nationality   18

Table 1:   Participants' Demographics   16-17

© Beth Rankin

Preface and acknowledgments:
Theo Gavrielides, IARS Founder & Director, July 2013

Rape, domestic violence and sexual abuse, forced marriage and forced adoption, female genital mutilation and forced sterilisation are all serious crimes that we have also acknowledged as human rights violations. However, an even more serious crime is society ignoring the realities of these offences, or not responding adequately to the needs of their victims.

I always feared that the power structures that exist within our governance systems and modern societies prioritise the utility of the few and principally those who already have a voice. At the same time, I always believed that true democracy and the values underlying it such as freedom, dignity and respect, should be measured not by economic success or the re-election of the party in government, but by how much those who have power, any power, share it with others and thus enabling them to pursue better lives.

I am particularly proud of this book and the larger project within which it is placed. It is an excellent reminder of why I set up IARS just over ten years ago. It is not good enough to watch passively other people's sufferings when we can spare some of our own 'power' to bring a better power balance in society. We do not need to be politicians or figures with decision-making authority to act. Speaking for myself, as a middle-class white man, I am already in a better place than other groups as they receive public services within a racially and gendered biased structural society. And let me be clear that when I use the term 'race' I place it within its sociological context to refer to the process of power that 'racialises' groups and identities. I am not interested in its biological interpretation, but in the power structures that the term is infused with as well as the interactionism meaning it gains through the existence of 'the other'. Racism is something that affects us all whether we see it now or subconsciously ignore it for our children. One of my favourite saying is "First it was the Jews, then it was the Blacks, then it was the Irish. Now it is you".

The book is based on a case study that has both a geographical and thematic focus. It aims to provide much needed evidence on the experiences of refugee and asylum seeking women who have been victims of abuse and power. The locus is London and the service areas that were investigated were health and legal. The findings are provocative and timely. The book also proceeds with a number of evidence-based solutions for government and its services, which have recently been extremely reactionary and political in their immigration policies. The voices of

Preface and acknowledgments

the women in this book should act as a reminder of the welcoming nature of British society and of its key characteristics of tolerance and inclusivity. "Where, after all, do universal human rights begin? In small places, close to home and so small that they cannot be seen on any map of the world. Yet they are the world of the individual person", as Eleanor Roosevelt reminds us.

Consistent with IARS' strapline for "Community-led Solutions for a Better Society" and in line with our core research methodology of producing user-led evidence, the study was led by a female group of refugee and asylum seeking community researchers. These are Sandra, Miriam, Mariam, Denise, Opeyemi, Prossy, Aisha, Sylvia, Mojgan, Sarah, Akberet, and Fatbardha. I cannot thank them enough for their hard work and commitment to the project. They worked voluntarily and against their personal challenges and life priorities.

I would also like to thank the 46 refugee and asylum seeking women who participated in this study; the project would not have been possible without them. We were touched by the honesty and openness with which they shared their experiences and hope that this book accurately represents their experiences. In the interests of confidentiality and research ethics they remain anonymous. While some were open about the gender related violence they experienced, others shared their experience as victims of persecution that related to their sexual orientation, political and societal status.

I am also extremely grateful to the 'gatekeeping organisations' who helped us to access research participants and arranged for us to come and speak to their service users. At IARS we acknowledge our limitations and hence we aim to build as many partnerships as possible with like-minded organisations that can help us achieve our charitable mission. The following organisations were particularly instrumental to us reaching our sample: Room to Heal, Migrant Refugee Community Forum (MRCF), British Red Cross, Migrant Right's Centre, IKWRO, The Holy Cross Centre Trust, IMECE, Barnet Refugee Service and the Iranian Association. We would also like to thank those professionals from 42 refugee organisations across the UK who took part in our scoping exercise into crisis points in service provision for refugee women.

I am particularly grateful to the author and lead researcher for the project Holly Challenger. Without her hard work, dedication, emotional investment and professionalism this book would not have materialised. At the time of writing this introduction, she is getting ready to move onto new and exciting projects. I hope that in a few years time she can look back with much pride for what she has achieved for IARS, the project, the women who were involved, for society. It is bit by

Preface and acknowledgments

bit and day by day that we make society better. It is not through large and expensive actions. That is why one of IARS' core organisational values is individual empowerment so that anyone who feels they can contribute to society, they do so in an equal and fair manner.

Nevertheless, even charities are not able to provide everything for free and therefore we are extremely grateful for the financial support that we received from Comic Relief who continues to support the larger project and its wider objectives. The book and the costs associated with it were also sponsored by Matrix Chambers while during the year we received small but numerous donations from individuals including a small amount from a charity run that Holly did. Running a charity with a primary task the collection of bottom up evidence and the carrying out of user-led research to change society is very hard in the current economic climate. Numerous were the nights when I lost faith only to wake up the next morning more determined to continue the course. My primary inspiration is my team and Holly is one example. For this project, I am also grateful to Rachel Cass and Hanna Sansom. Thanks also go to Dr. Margaret Greenfields from IDRICS of Buckinghamshire New University.

We have a long way to go before we can safely claim that violence against women is eradicated. Persistent racial and gender inequalities and the control of power must be prioritised and this book makes a contribution by allowing those directly affected to speak up. I hope that it can be used as a lever for change.

Professor Theo Gavrielides

Preface and acknowledgments

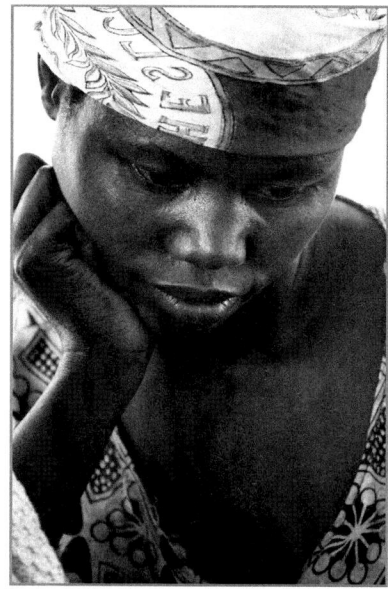

© Steve Evans

Foreword: Lynne Berry OBE, July 2013

Director: Public Benefit, Chief Executive: WRVS (2007-11),
Chief Executive: General Social Care Council (2001-7), Chief Executive: Equal Opportunities Commission (1999-2011), Executive Director Charity Commission (1996-99)

The latest government figures indicate that annually Britain receives around 5,500 asylum claims from women who face persecution. Almost 40% of them were persecuted simply because of their gender. This referred to instances of repeat rape, sexual violence, domestic violence, adultery, female genital mutilation, trafficking, forced marriage, forced sterilisation and forced adoption. 74% of those claiming asylum were mothers while the majority came from Pakistan, followed by Iran, Nigeria, Sri Lanka, China, Zimbabwe, Libya and Eritrea. Any crime should be a concern for society. However, certain crimes that target our humanity and those who are most vulnerable should raise even more serious concerns as they shake the very foundations of our society.

This book could not be more timely as its exclusive focus is the investigation of the experiences of one of the most vulnerable groups in modern British society. Asylum seeking women who have been, and in most cases continue to be, victims of violence and sexual abuse face multiple challenges and are exposed to higher risks for discrimination. Most of the time, this discrimination relates to the hidden biases that we all carry. However, there are occasions where the system and public services simply fail to respond to their individual needs and circumstances.

Of course, the issue of violence against women is much wider. In fact, last year around 1.2 million women suffered domestic abuse, over 400,000 women were sexually assaulted, 60,000 women were raped and thousands more were stalked. Fewer than 1 in 4 people who suffer abuse at the hands of their partner - and only around 1 in 10 women who experience serious sexual assault - report it to the police.

We now have a dedicated international day that reminds humanity of its commitment to eliminate violence against women. In 2010, on the first anniversary the coalition government took the opportunity to publish its strategic vision and in March 2011 the relevant department published its action plan. Following the "Stern Review" in 2010 on the handling of rape and sexual violence complaints by public authorities, it became clear that modern Britain had a long way to go before we could safely claim that our public services, and by extension our society, is responsive to this persistent human rights issue. The government's plan was

Foreword

updated in 2012 and then again in 2013. This showed how continuously changing the issue is. It also highlighted the need to remain connected with the realities of the victims and the involved perpetrators.

The truth is that the literature is faced with an important gap. The evidence documenting the lived experiences of women survivors is scant. This is due to the sensitive nature of these cases as well as risks around ethics, participation and bias. The evidence on the lived experiences of women who are survivors of these abuses and are from a refugee and asylum seeking background is almost nonexistent. That is why this book is unique and is indeed a welcomed contribution to the literature. The fact that legal and health services were prioritised as the foci of investigation should indicate the key areas of concern for these women. The current reforms to the NHS and legal aid services are one more reason why this publication is so timely.

The book also takes an additional bold step. It has constructed its evidence base by involving the user directly. As per IARS' commitment for user led evidence and its vision for "community led solutions for a better society", the fieldwork that was carried out for this book was conducted by a group of refugee and asylum seeking women who had experienced gender related violence. Recruiting, empowering and genuinely enabling this group to conduct research and through this publication acquire a much needed and long overdue voice is worth commending. The fact that these women supported the project on a voluntary basis while dealing with their own personal challenges is another indicator of commitment, and indeed hope.

I want to congratulate them as well as the author of this book. Acknowledgement should also be given to Comic Relief and Matrix Chambers which funded the work and this publication. Innovative projects such as this one are associated with a number of risks that funders tend to avoid. However, it is by believing in the abilities of the people that we aim to genuinely support and indeed by taking risks that true progress can be made. This is also to the credit of IARS and Dr. Theo Gavrielides who has created an international reputation for genuinely involving the user in the production of evidence based recommendations for social policy and practice.

Lynne Berry OBE

Introduction and impetus for the book

1.1 Introduction

This study, undertaken by IARS between May 2012 and May 2013 with funding from Comic Relief, investigates the impact of gender and experiences of gender-related violence on the experiences of refugee women[1] in the UK passing through the asylum process and accessing key services. It provides insight into refugee women's experiences of GP and solicitors' services in Greater London in order to identify whether a more tailored approach to working with this group is needed.

This study was carried out as the result of the experiences of IARS' volunteers, who, as refugee women, had personally experienced difficulties in receiving the support they needed from professionals in mainstream services as a result of suffering from Post-Traumatic Stress Disorder (PTSD). Existing research highlights the problems refugee women face in receiving the support they need from mainstream services, particularly those who have experienced gender-related violence (Phillimore et al, 2007). A gap was identified in existing literature around refugee women's perspectives on accessing mainstream services in the UK and a scoping exercise with professionals in the refugee sector identified refugee women's interaction with GPs and solicitors as significant crisis points. The scoping exercise, undertaken with forty two professionals from the refugee sector, found that both GPs and solicitors were in need of extra training and support on how to sensitively work with this group.

Refugee women are a particularly vulnerable group as a result of race and gender inequalities, which continue to persist in our society. The Commission for Race Equality's 'legacy' document 'A lot done, a lot to do' (2007:1) states that Britain is 'still a place of inequality, exclusion and isolation' and in their report 'The Gender Agenda', the Equal Opportunities Commission (2007) outlines the extent to which gender inequality continues to exist in the UK. The former Secretary General of the United Nations, Kofi Annan (1999) described violence against women as one of 'the most pervasive' forms human rights violation. The intersection of race and gender inequalities, combined with experiences of gender-related violence as well as difficulties as a result of their immigration statuses mean that refugee women are a particularly marginalised group in British society.

Introduction and impetus for the book

The mental and physical health problems often associated with forms of gender-related persecution[2] means that the needs of refugee women are often multiple and complex. A significant number of refugee women in the UK can be assumed to have experienced a form of gender-related violence or persecution in their country of origin. This group are also particularly vulnerable to sexual violence whilst they are living in the UK (Refugee Council, 2009). Therefore a gender-sensitive approach to working with refugee women is of paramount importance in order to identify gender specific support needs as early as possible when a refugee woman first comes into contact with a service provider/professional.

GPs and solicitors play a significant role in the welfare of refugee women in the UK; they help the women in matters of life and liberty. Solicitors are crucial to refugee women's claims for asylum and GPs are key to treating the mental and physical health problems that may have been inflicted in their home country. Almost all refugee women come into contact with GPs and solicitors soon after their arrival in the UK. These professionals can play a significant role in identifying refugee women's support needs and signposting or referring them to other services.

By examining refugee women's experiences of these two areas of service provision *from the women's perspective*, it is possible to identify aspects of service delivery that could be altered or improved to ensure adequate support and to identify what a 'gender-sensitive approach' to working with this vulnerable group might look like for GPs and solicitors.

The timing of this report is pertinent as there is a great deal of movement and interest around gender-related violence at present, with the Home Secretary, Theresa May, dedicated to this issue. The UK is a State party to the UN Convention on the Elimination of All Forms of Discrimination against Women (CEDAW) and therefore has accepted a legal obligation to counteract discrimination against women. The Major of London, Boris Johnson, has implemented a strategy for ending violence against women, 'The Way Forward', which aims to support boroughs to develop local violence against women strategies across London. The UK coalition government's new action plan published in 2013 as part of their strategy entitled *Call to End Violence Against Women and Girls* sets out their commitment to a gender-sensitive asylum system and to support victims of sexual violence more generally, ensuring they 'receive a good consistent level of service across England and Wales' (HM Government, 2013:20). The action plan identifies the need for asylum-seeking women who are victims of gender-related violence to

Introduction and impetus for the book

be signposted to appropriate services and support. It also sets out to raise awareness of the prevalence of violence against women and girls in refugee communities amongst practitioners and decision makers (ibid:54). However, for services to be sensitive to the needs of refugee women who have been victims of gender-related violence, it is vital to consult with the women about their experiences of key professionals to gain a greater understanding of their needs. This research therefore seeks to provide insight into what refugee women themselves require from GPs and solicitors; what makes them feel safe and listened to; and, what makes it easier for them to access the services and support they need.

It is an opportune moment to consider refugee women's experiences of GP and solicitor services in light of the changes to these two areas of service provision brought about by the Legal Aid, Sentencing and Punishment of Offenders Act, 2012 and the Health and Social Care Act, 2012. This is a time of transition as the impact of these pieces of legislation on refugee women's experiences of these services largely remain to be seen. This report aims to bring to the fore the voices of this marginalised group in the hope that their needs will be addressed in this changing policy landscape.

1.2 Book Structure

This report contains a literature review on the impact of gender and gender-related persecution on the experiences of refugee women in the UK and the key crisis points and gaps in service provision where there is a need for a more gender-sensitive approach to working with this group (see Chapter three). The literature review addresses topics such as the impact of gender-related persecution on refugee women's physical and mental health, the particular difficulties they face during Home Office interviews and the problems they face as a result of homelessness and destitution. Chapter two presents the methodology of the study and provides an overview of the participants.

Following a scoping exercise with 46 questionnaires that were completed by refugee and asylum seeking specialist organisations, chapters four to six present the findings and analysis of semi-structured qualitative interviews with refugee women about their experiences of GP and solicitors' services. Chapter four focuses on refugee women's interaction with GP services and explores their experiences of registering with a GP practice, the difficulties they experience as a result of language barriers and the use of interpreters in GP appointments. Chapter five

Introduction and impetus for the book

discusses participants' experiences of accessing solicitor services and the impact of detention and dispersal on their experiences of this service. The prevalence of refugee women paying for legal help from solicitors is depicted as well as the problems they face in communicating with solicitors about the progress of asylum claims and the impact of the presence of children during solicitor appointments. Chapter six thematically explores the common issues that refugee women face with both GPs and solicitors. The chapter outlines the crucial factors for effective interactions with both sets of professionals in relation to the participants' underlying mental health problems and their experiences of gender-related violence.

The discussion and recommendations of the study are presented in Chapter seven. This final chapter uses the evidence gathered from the fieldwork to formulate the crucial elements of a gender-sensitive approach to working with this group of women and locates the perspectives of the participants within the current policy context of ensuring that refugee women who are victims of gender-related violence receive appropriate support and also to raise awareness amongst practitioners of the prevalence of gender-related violence in refugee communities.

Notes

1. The term 'refugee woman' is used henceforth to refer to those women who have been granted refugee status or Indefinite Leave to remain, those in the process of applying for asylum and those who have been refused asylum in the UK.
2. The term gender-related persecution' refers to the experiences of women who are persecuted because they are women. The UNHRC (2002:2) defines this term as referring 'to a range of different experiences in which gender is a relevant consideration' (UNHCR, 2002:2). This report uses the term to mean either the reason for or the form of persecution may be related to gender.

Research Strategy

2.1 Methodology and IARS' user-led, action research ethos

The study used a process of triangulation to investigate the impact of gender and experiences of gender-related violence on the experiences of refugee women in the UK passing through the asylum process and accessing key services. This included a desk-based review of existing literature; a scoping exercise with professionals in the refugee sector; and qualitative fieldwork interviews with refugee women living in London about their experiences of GP and solicitor services.

Having conducted a literature review on the impact of gender and gender-related violence on refugee women's experiences in the UK, a scoping exercise was carried out into the crisis points and gaps in service provision for refugee women. This scoping exercise involved consulting with forty two professionals from third sector organisations working with refugee women across the UK. This consultation identified particular problems with refugee women's interactions with GPs and solicitors. These problems were seen to be compounded by the importance of these professionals and their role as gatekeepers to other services for refugee women. They were therefore chosen as the focus of the fieldwork phase of the study.

During the fieldwork phase of the study, a combination of individual and group face-to-face semi-structured interviews were conducted with forty six refugee women living in London between December 2012 and February 2013. By carrying out group interviews as well as individual interviews we were able to increase the number of participants involved in the study. The structure of group and individual interviews remained largely the same as the interviewer remained 'the focal point of the communication' (Denscombe, 2007: 78).

Due to the vulnerability of the sample and the difficulties refugee women face with disclosure of sensitive personal information, it was deemed appropriate to adopt a peer-led approach for this study, which supported refugee women to undertake interviews with their peer group.[3] A principle reason for adopting this research model was so that there was a commonality of experience between interviewers and participant (Greenfield & Ryder, 2012), which created an empathetic and supportive environment and better enabled participants to communicate their experiences. A group of twelve refugee women were recruited as peer researchers. These women were from a range of nationalities and

Research Strategy

religions so that there would be scope for participants to be given a choice of being interviewed by a researcher from her own country or religion.

The volunteers were recruited through various refugee community organisations and specialist refugee charities across London and were a mix of those who had been granted Indefinite Leave to Remain and those in the process of seeking asylum. The volunteering opportunity aimed to increase the refugee women volunteers' sense of well-being and control in their lives by developing their ability to talk about their own past experiences with their peer group, improve their knowledge and understanding of policy and law around the asylum process and improve their levels of self-confidence.

IARS has a strong track record of conducting user-led action research, which supports individuals to shape decision-making. This methodological approach embodies the charity's aim to enable communities to generate solutions to specific problems that they face and to give everyone a chance to forge a safer, fairer and more inclusive society.

This peer-led approach 'empowers researchers and research participants by enabling their 'voices' to be heard' and is based on the Participatory Action Research (PAR) model (Greenfields, 2013). The group of twelve refugee women attended a series of training programmes in research methods, research ethics and how to undertake individual and group interviews. Through a process of empowerment and by reflecting on their own life experiences, the peer researchers led on the design of the study's research tools and fed into the analysis process.

A primary concern was to ensure the welfare of the peer researchers, who were themselves vulnerable, most of them with outstanding asylum claims, mental health problems and insecure living arrangements. For this reason, peer researchers were provided with individual mentors to support them through the fieldwork activities. Peer researchers also attended group sessions on preparing themselves for conducting interviews with other refugee women experiencing distress and were provided with good practice guidance on protecting their own welfare during the fieldwork process. Each peer researcher conducted their first interview under the supervision of an IARS staff member and thereafter conducted interviews in pairs with another trained volunteer. In exceptional circumstances where participants were known by the peer researcher, an interview would be conducted with just one interviewer present. On the few occasions when peer researchers were unable to attend a fieldwork activity, interviews were carried out by a female IARS staff member.

Research Strategy

When pairing peer researchers with other refugee women to interview, consideration was given to cultural sensitivities that might affect the interview process. Great care was also taken to ensure the welfare of all research participants. Peer researchers were alerted to issues around vulnerable adult protection and instructed to report all concerns about participants to the project coordinator. Participants were taken through an information sheet providing them with information about the project before the interview commenced, were asked to give their informed consent to participate in the study and told that they could stop the interview at any time.

The sample were accessed using a combination of convenience and snowball sampling techniques and all participants were required to be over eighteen years and to be either a current or former asylum-seeker in the UK. A large proportion of participants were accessed through refugee and community organisations across London, who referred refugee women to be interviewed for the study. The organisations that referred refugee women to be interviewed for this study were: Room To Heal, Migrant Resource Centre, Migrant Refugee Community Forum (MRCF), The Holy Cross Centre Trust (HCCT), The British Red Cross, Brent Refugee Service and IMECE Women's Centre. These organisations were sent information about the research and met with the project coordinator to discuss the nature of the research in more detail. Interviews were arranged by the referral organisations and interviews took place at the referral organisations' premises as these were locations familiar to the participants. An advantage of the peer-led approach also enabled us to access refugee women using a snowballing method of promoting the study through the personal networks of the peer researchers and seven women were referred using this technique. This enabled us to reach those refugee women who may not have been in contact with specialist refugee support services. In these cases, researchers referred women they knew and believed might be suitable to participate to the project coordinator, who assessed their suitability and arranged the logistics of the interview.

During the interviews participants were asked to provide basic demographic information, such as their country of origin, immigration status and number of children, if any. A pre-interview questionnaire asked them to assess their level of English when they first arrived in the UK as well as their competency at the time of interview and also asked them to divulge any mental or physical health conditions, which aimed to explore the prevalence of Post-Traumatic Stress Disorder (PTSD) and anxiety and depression amongst this group. A semi-structured interview then followed, which explored refugee women's experiences of GPs and solicitors. The women were asked about their experiences of registering and accessing GP services and solicitors, their level of satisfaction with both services, any particularly positive and negative experiences they may have had with both groups of professionals and the impact of dispersal on their experiences of these areas of service provision.

Confidentiality

Due to the vulnerability of the sample group, it was important to ensure that their involvement in the research did not expose them to 'danger or make them any more vulnerable'(Greenfields, 2013:10). All names of those who were involved have been removed and replaced with codes and participants have not been referenced in relation to their country of origin. Participants' names were not attached to pre-interview questionnaires or to interview transcripts. Interviews were recorded by the peer researchers and transcribed by the project coordinator and all recordings have subsequently been deleted. Peer researchers were required to sign a confidentiality agreement and were prepared for sensitivities that may arise when interviewing refugee women they knew. Special consideration was given to confidentiality issues when peer researchers interviewed refugee women who were known to them personally; participants were always given a choice of being interviewed by another peer researcher who they did not know and were reassured that any issues discussed during the interview would remain confidential.

Limitations

Twenty-one interviews were conducted with the help of interpreters. Where interpreters were used the refugee women's exact words may not have been recorded. Group interviews provided a way to increase the number of participants involved in the research, but in some cases this meant that some women did not answer every question required as researchers would run out of time and have to cut interviews short. Interviews conducted with groups of refugee women also collected less detailed information about individual participants as each woman had to be given the opportunity to speak.

The sample was limited to refugee women living in the Greater London area. With the majority of asylum seekers dispersed out of London and the South East (unless there are extenuating circumstances) a limitation is placed on the project and will in turn affect the findings of the fieldwork. However, even though the majority of asylum seekers are dispersed away from the capital, research shows that many move back to London whilst waiting for a decision from UKBA (Robinson,

Research Strategy

Anderson & Musterd, 2003). Consequently the sample includes those refugee women who were not dispersed outside of London as well as those who were dispersed to different regions across the UK and then returned independently to the capital.

As a result of a using convenience sampling methodology and accessing refugee women to participate in this study through 'gate-keepers' such as community organisations, some nationalities are over represented in the sample because of certain organisations' willingness to participate. Involving a representative cross-section of nationalities of refugee women in London proved difficult as certain communities were unwilling to promote the opportunity to their members due to the sensitivity of the topic, despite reassurances regarding the anonymity of participants and the nature of the peer-led approach.

2.2 Overview of the participants & sampling strategy

Forty six refugee women were interviewed as part of this study. Most of these women were asylum-seekers with just eight having been granted refugee status, seven having been given Leave to Remain and seven granted British citizenship.

The sample, all of whom were over eighteen, included twenty two women who had come to the UK alone and twenty four who had claimed asylum with family members, as displayed in Table 1 overleaf.

Figure 1: Immigration status and number of research participants

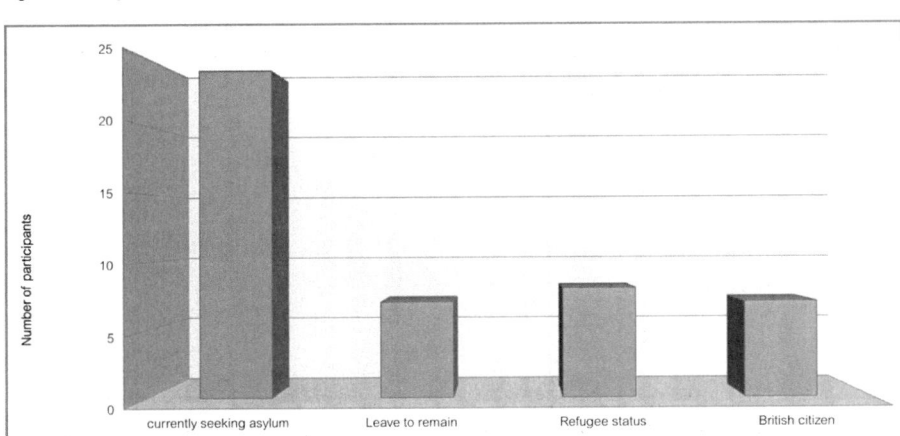

Table 1: Participants' Demographics

Participant ID	Length of time in the UK	Age	Sought asylum alone or with family
PO01	8 years	26-50 (29)	26-50 (29)
KC01	5 years	50-80	50-80
KC02	9 years	18-25	18-25
KC03	6 years	26-50	26-50
KC04	8 years	26-50	26-50
WC01	9 years	26-50 (37)	26-50 (37)
WC02	10 years	26-50 (28)	26-50 (28)
DM01	unknown	26-50	26-50
LH01	9 years	26-50	26-50
DN03	9 years	26-50	26-50
IN01	9 years	26-50 (38)	26-50 (38)
IN02	23 years	26-50 (47)	26-50 (47)
IN03	15 years	26-50 (40)	26-50 (40)
IN04	20 years	26-50 (42)	26-50 (42)
IN05	18 years	50-80 (57)	50-80 (57)
IN08	11 years	26-50 (45)	26-50 (45)
IN09	23 years	26-50 (48)	26-50 (48)
DN02	14 years	26-50	26-50
DN01	11 years	26-50	26-50
CL01	4 years	26-50	26-50
LH02	10 years	26-50	26-50
OT02	8 years	26-50 (26)	26-50 (26)
OT03	12 years	26-50 (32)	26-50 (32)
FY01	unknown	26-50	26-50
FY02	unknown	26-50	26-50
FY03	6months	26-50	26-50
FY04	unknown	26-50	26-50
FY05	unknown	26-50	26-50
FY06	unknown	26-50	26-50
FY07	unknown	26-50	26-50

Research Strategy

Table 1: Participants' Demographics *(continued...)*

Participant ID	Length of time in the UK	Age	Sought asylum alone or with family
FY08	unknown	26-50	26-50
FY09	unknown	26-50	26-50
FY10	unknown	26-50	26-50
FY11	unknown	26-50	26-50
FY12	unknown	26-50	26-50
CN01	10 years	50-80 (63)	50-80 (63)
CN02	14 years	50-80 (72)	50-80 (72)
CN03	20 years	50-80 (80)	50-80 (80)
CN04	12 years	50-80 (71)	50-80 (71)
HY01	unknown	26-50	26-50
HY02	unknown	26-50	26-50
HY03	unknown	26-50	26-50
HY04	unknown	26-50	26-50
HY05	unknown	26-50	26-50
HY06	unknown	26-50	26-50
HY07	unknown	26-50	26-50

Of those research participants who divulged how long they had been in the UK, only two had been in the UK for less than five years and the majority had been living in this country for ten to fifteen years. Overall, sixteen nationalities were covered by the research. The range of nationalities included can be seen in Figure two below overleaf.

Women's mental and physical wellbeing

Most of the women who participated said that they suffered with mental health problems, with 75% of them reporting suffering from depression, 83% said they regularly experienced stress and anxiety and 40% were aware that they had been diagnosed with Post Traumatic Stress Disorder (PTSD).

The participants related their states of mental health to the trauma they had experienced in their home country, as well as their post-migratory experiences, including their anxiety surrounding their asylum claim and the isolation they had

Research Strategy

Figure 2: Participants' Nationality

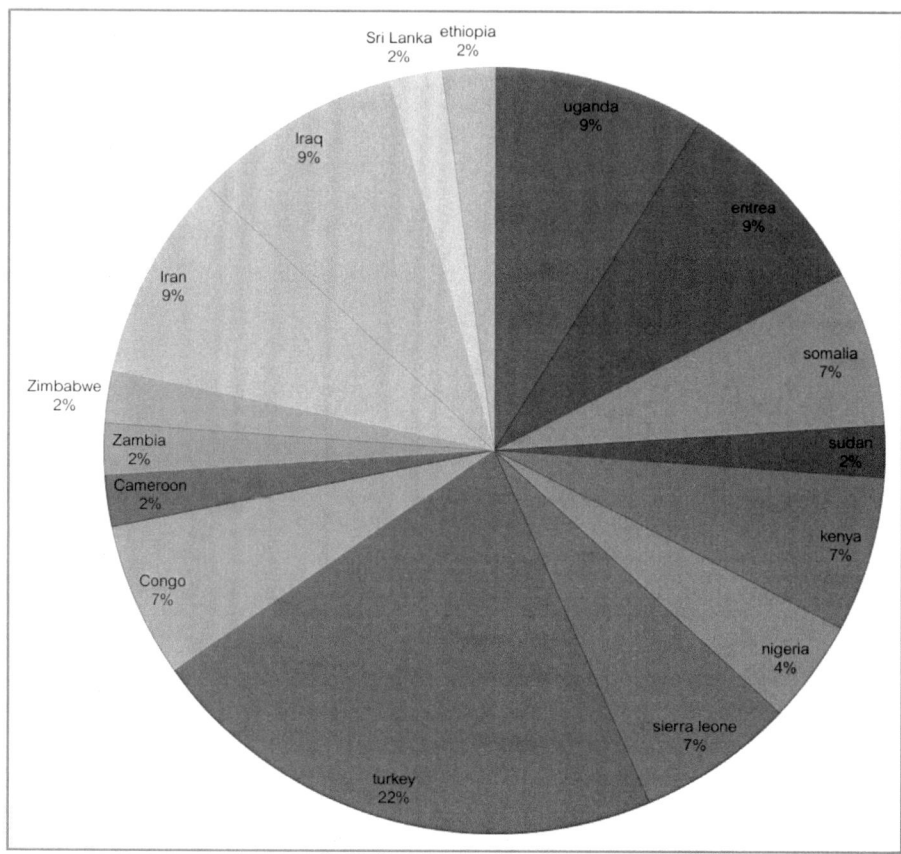

experienced in the UK. One woman openly disclosed the suicidal feelings she had experienced:

> *I was so depressed and sometimes you feel like, you have this problem, you have this, you have this and I was feeling, this is not the world for me to live. And this is things which is...I tried to do bad things to myself (DT01)*

The majority of the women described themselves as being in a poor state of health and detailed numerous physical health complaints. One woman told us that she had gynaecological problems as a result of being raped in her country of origin. Many women displayed high levels of anxiety around their physical health and four women started crying during the interviews when discussing their health conditions. One participant related the strong correlation between her mental and physical wellbeing:

When I was in detention...I started to have problems with my bowels...and the doctor said it's because you're stressed out and you should see a counsellor (PO01)

This young woman also told us that her hair has begun to fall out, she believed as a result of stress. Another participant detailed the difficulty of coping with severe health problems whilst being an asylum-seeker:

Obviously, when you are an asylum-seeker and you are ill at the same time... .Like now, they are saying they need to remove my womb. I am a woman, I need, this is what sometimes you don't want to think about it. It's too much (DN01)

This woman's ability to cope with the strain and anxiety associated with her physical health problems was negatively affected by her situation as an asylum-seeker.

Living situation

Whilst 90% of those interviewed had not been dispersed outside of London, many of them had moved around London a great deal and recounted living in very uncertain housing situations. Five of the women said that they had to rely on friends to house them and that they have no permanent address and spent weeks/months at a time staying with different friends across London. One seventy two year old woman told us that she was living on the streets and had to beg to buy food. Another woman being housed with her young daughter in a bed and breakfast by the local authority told us that she did not know where she would be living from one week to the next and had to live out of a suitcase. Those housed by UKBA also said that they are regularly required to change accomodation.

Research Strategy

© IARS

The impact of gender and experiences of gender-related persecution on refugee and asylum seeking women in the UK: A review of the literature

3.1 Refugee and asylum-seeking women in the UK

In both the UK and Europe as a whole, one third of people seeking asylum in their own right (i.e. not as a dependent) are women (Cheikh Ali, Querton & Soulard, 2012:8). According to Home Office (2012) statistics, 5,392 women claimed asylum in their own right in the UK in 2011 compared to 14,460 men. A significant number of women also apply for asylum as dependents on an annual basis. In the UK in 2011, 38% (3,388) of applications for asylum made by dependents were women (Home Office, 2012). The situation differs across EU nations, for instance in 2010 France received the most number of female asylum seekers (14,016) and Hungary the least (308) (Cheikh Ali *et al.*, 2012:24).

Home Office statistics for 2012 reveal that the most common countries of origin of women seeking asylum in the UK in 2011 were: Pakistan (1,598), Iran (854), Nigeria (563), Sri Lanka (527), China (465), Zimbabwe (384), Libya (372), Eritrea (362), Somalia (323), The Gambia (241), Afghanistan (232) (Home Office, 2012).

Many refugee women are mothers. Of the women surveyed for Dumper's (2002a:1) report for Refugee Action, *Is it Safe Here?*, 74% said they were mothers (a third of whom were separated from their children) and more than two thirds were here without a spouse because they had been 'widowed or separated by the conflict from which they were forced to flee'. This is corroborated by Dorling, Girma and Walter (2012:15) who claim that 'nearly a third of the women in our research told us that they have children in their country of origin'.

Many women seek asylum for the same reasons as men; because they have experienced persecution due to their political opinion, race, religion, nationality, or membership of a particular social group (Dorling et al., 2012:6). In a study conducted by Dorling et al (2012:5), over a third of the women interviewed stated that they had faced persecution for the same reasons associated with male asylum seekers. However, in the same study, 39% of women said that they had

The impact of gender and experiences of gender-related persecution

experienced persecution because of their gender (ibid).

Refugees are not a homogenous group and have differing needs and experiences. However, Van de Veer (1998) classifies eight types of common experiences for refugees of both genders including political repression, detention, torture and rape, disappearance of relatives, separation, loss, hardship and exile.

3.2 **Gender-related persecution**

Over the past 10 years it has become widely acknowledged that women are particularly vulnerable to gender-related forms of persecution, including rape and sexual violence, domestic violence, adultery, female genital mutilation (FGM), trafficking, discrimination, forced marriage, forced sterilisation and forced abortion (Querton, 2012:7). Many women fear persecution because of their gender 'including because they refuse to conform to established gender roles within a given society' (ibid). The UN High Commissioner for Refugees (2002) defines gender-related asylum claims as having 'typically encompassed, although by no means limited to, acts of sexual violence, family/domestic violence, coerced family planning, female genital mutilation, punishment for transgression of social mores, and discrimination against homosexuals'. Many women are not persecuted because of their gender, but because of their religion or ethnicity. Nevertheless, this persecution is more likely to take the form of rape or sexual violence (Dorling et al., 2012:6).

According to research carried out by the Refugee Council (2009:4), 'a substantial proportion of refugee women arriving in the UK can be assumed to have survived rape, attempted rape, other sexual violence or sexual exploitation' because many women who seek asylum in the UK come from countries 'with high levels of sexual violence' and from countries where 'sexual violence by security forces has been institutionalised'. The Refugee Council's *The Vulnerable Women's Project* worked with 153 refugee women between 2006 and 2008 (ibid). Of these women 76% had been raped, either in their country of origin or in the UK, 15% had become pregnant as result of being raped, 22% had been sexually abused and 35% had suffered some form of violence (ibid:9). As this project worked primarily with refugee women who had been subjected to sexual violence, it is doubtful that these statistics are representative of the female refugee population in the UK as a whole. Furthermore, the Home Office does not make public statistics relating to the types of persecution women flee. Dorling et al.'s (2012) recent study may offer a more representative figure as their sample included women with a diverse range of experiences. Of the 70 women interviewed for this project the most common reason

The impact of gender and experiences of gender-related persecution

given for the persecution they had experienced was 'because I am a woman' and nearly half the women had been raped (just under a third by police, soldiers or prison guards) (ibid:6). From this report, it can be deduced that many refugee women in the UK will have experienced gender-related persecution and violence.

In addition to acts of sexual violence, gender-related violence also encompasses persecution and discrimination as a result of an individual's sexual orientation. However, across Europe few asylum claims by lesbians have been reported and a lack of data exists regarding Lesbian Bisexual, trans and intersex asylum-seekers (Jansen & Spijkerboer, 2011).

Women are also trafficked to the UK, primarily for sex work (Craig, Gaus, Wilkinson, Skrivankova, & McQuade., 2007:50). Trafficking for sex work is a form of gender-related persecution as laid out by the UNHCR (UNHCR, 2002). In 2006, the Home Office estimated that 400 women had been trafficked into prostitution in the UK, although this is believed to be a 'serious underestimate' (ibid: 50). Women who have been trafficked to the UK have often experienced physical and emotional violence including rape, torture and beatings (Zimmerman, Hossain, Yun, Roche, Morison & Watts, 2006).

Well-being of refugee women

As a result of experiences in their country of origin, refugees of both sexes typically experience additional health problems in comparison to the rest of the UK population. These are compounded 'by poor access to healthcare and the dangerous and stressful journey to the UK' (Burnett & Peel, 2001a). A worldwide study found that refugees have higher rates of psychopathological disorder compared to non-refugee groups (Porter & Haslam, 2005).

Mental and physical health complaints are common among female refugees. Research carried out on behalf of the Asylum Support Appeals Project (ASAP) entitled *Barriers to Support Appeals for Asylum-Seeking Women* reveals that 'More than three-quarters of the appellants [asylum-seeking women] had mental or physical health problems covering a wide range of ailments, including HIV, renal failure, post-traumatic stress disorder, depression, high blood pressure, vitamin deficiency and back pain' (Hickey, 2011:5).

Physical impact of gender-related persecution

In addition to the health problems faced by refugees of both sexes face, women who are victims of sexual violence experience added physical and mental health problems (Refugee Council, 2009). The physical consequences of sexual violence

The impact of gender and experiences of gender-related persecution

include pregnancy, gynaecological complications and sexually transmitted diseases, including HIV/AIDS (Jewkes, Sen & Garcia-Morena, 2002). It has been noted that due to the stigma and taboo surrounding HIV/AIDS many victims of sexual violence 'may not voice their fears about the possibility of HIV infection' (Burnett & Peel, 2001b). Of the women and girls who have undergone Female Genital Mutilation (FGM), 10% experience short-term complications such as haemorrhage, shock and infection (Momoh, 2005:7) and a further 25% 'die in the long term, as a result of recurrent urinary and vaginal infections and complications during childbirth, such as severe bleeding and obstructed labour' (ibid:8).

The physical manifestation of mental distress, known as somatisation, has also been described in relation to female refugees and asylum seekers as they 'may come from cultures where somatisation is common...or where there is a strong cultural prohibition against mental distress' (Refugee Council, 2009:29). As a result, refugee women may present physical health complaints, which are rooted in psychological distress.

Mental health impact of gender-related persecution

Research carried out for the World Health Organisation notes that 'physical injuries are not always a consequence [of sexual violence]' but that 'the more common consequences of sexual violence are those related to...mental health and social well-being' (Jewkes, Sen & Garcia-Morena, 2002:161). Studies have shown that women refugees are more likely than men to suffer from Post-Traumatic Stress Disorder (PTSD), depression and anxiety (Gerritsen, Bramsen, Deville, Van Willigen, Hovens & Van der Ploeg, 2006). PTSD is commonly associated with victims of sexual violence, along with avoidance symptoms and feelings of shame (Bögner, Herlihy & Brewin, 2007). Anxiety, nightmares, flashbacks, depression and reduced self-esteem are also recognised as common psychological symptoms of rape or sexual assault (Refugee Council, 2009:4). It is thought that because of the way the brain copes with traumatic memories, those who have experienced a traumatic incident may 'be unable to recall aspects of what happened' (ibid:6). The prevalence of mental health problems amongst this group is of considerable concern due to ethnic inequalities present in the provision of mental health services to BME groups (Mind, 2013).

Mental health impact of the asylum process

Mental health problems have been correlated with the experience of going through the asylum process. Dorling et al (2012:22) state, 'More than half of the women in our research contemplated suicide after being told they were not being given asylum'. Furthermore, Silove, Sinnerbrink, Field, Manicavasagar & Steel (1997:351) found, 'a diagnosis of PTSD was associated with greater exposure to *post-migration* trauma, delays in processing refugee applications, difficulties in dealing with immigration officials, obstacles to employment, racial discrimination, and loneliness and boredom'.

Mental health and life in the UK

Experiences of life in the UK have been linked to mental health problems amongst refugee women. In Dumper's (2002a:17) study 25% of participants stated that they have been diagnosed as suffering from psychological problems since arriving in the UK and 62% said they are kept awake by nightmares, depression or anxiety. Phillimore, Ergün, Goodson, Hennessy (2007:6) argue, 'experiences within the UK are often viewed by refugees as more detrimental to their mental health than the atrocities they underwent in their countries of origin'.

3.3 **Claiming asylum**

Refugee Convention and UK case law

Refugee status can be granted if there is a well-founded fear of persecution on the five grounds set out in the *Convention Relating to the Status of Refugees* (UN General Assembly, 1951): race, religion, nationality, political opinion, or membership of a particular social group. The Convention does not include gender as one of the grounds on which it is possible to be recognised as a refugee. It has been claimed that this has resulted in a gender-biased system and concerns about the impact of international refugee law on women's claims for asylum have been raised regularly over the past 10 years (Cheikh Ali et al., 2012:9). It has been contended that 'the curtailment of women's rights through practices such as domestic violence, forced marriage and female genital mutilation have traditionally been thought of as issues that are simply not covered by the Convention grounds of race, religion, political opinion and so on' (Dorling *et al.*, 2012:16). However, over the past 10 years progress in the UK higher courts means that it is now accepted that there are particular forms of persecution that are gender-specific[4] (Dorling *et al.*, 2012:16).

Developments in case law have improved the experiences of some women claiming asylum in this country. For example, the 1998 case of *Furundzija* (*The Prosecutor v. Anto Furundzija*, 1998) recognised that rape could amount to torture

The impact of gender and experiences of gender-related persecution

and the 1999 case of *Shah and Islam* (*Shah and Islam v. SSHD*, 1999) established that gender can constitute a 'particular social group'. In the 2006 case of *Fornah* (*K and Fornah v SSHD*, 2006) the House of Lords held that FGM was persecution and 'an extreme and cruel expression of male dominance' and the 2009 case of *MK (Lesbians) Albania v. Secretary of State for the Home Department* stated that lesbians can constitute a particular social group.

UK Border Agency initial decision-making

In order to encourage a gender-sensitive interpretation of the 1951 Refugee Convention the United Nations High Commission for Refugees (1991) produced guidelines in 1991 and 2002 to assist nations in considering claims relating to gender. In 2004 the UK Border Agency (UKBA) adopted an Asylum Instruction for case workers on *Gender Issues in the Asylum Claim*, which provides information on the type of persecution and discrimination someone might face on account of their gender and how to take gender into consideration when looking at the five Convention grounds in the Refugee Convention (UK Border Agency, 2010). Concerning the situation across Europe, there is no consistency regarding the adoption of gender guidelines across other EU member states. For example, Belgium and Italy do not have gender specific guidelines, but have instead developed alternative guidance material and France, Hungary and Spain, 'have neither national gender guidelines nor alternative gender-specific guidance' (Cheikh Ali *et al*, 2012:34).

Despite the implementation of gender guidelines in the UK, concern has been expressed by many that these guidelines are not being fully observed by UKBA staff (Hobson, Cox & Sagovsky, 2008a: 42). Muggeridge and Maman's (2011:66) study for Asylum Aid, *Unsustainable: The Quality of Initial Decision-Making in Women's Asylum Claims*, suggests that the progress made in the UK higher courts is not reflected in UKBA practice and that 'the majority of women's claims were simply disbelieved by UKBA case owners'. One of the key findings of this piece of research is that 'UKBA ignored PSG [the ground of membership of a Particular Social Group] entirely in the majority of cases based solely on gender-related persecution, and decided that no Refugee Convention Ground had been engaged' (ibid:6). A thematic review of gender issues in asylum claims conducted by UKBA's Quality Audit and Development Team concluded, 'if there was more than one Convention ground at play, case owners side-lined the gender-related grounds' (Querton, 2012:26). It also found 'a lack of investigation in cases involving domestic violence and whether an applicant's gender would affect her ability to seek state protection' (Querton, 2012:26).

The impact of gender and experiences of gender-related persecution

A report carried out by Independent Chief Inspector of the UK Border Agency, John Vine, *The Use of Country of Origin Information in deciding asylum applications* (2011:3) asserts '17% of reasons for refusal letters (12 cases) from our file sample showed either the selective use of country information or unjustified assertions based on the evidence available. Over 13% of reasons for refusal letters (7 cases) included country information which was, at best, tangential to the issues relevant to the asylum claim' (ibid). Furthermore, Home Office (2011b) statistics show that nearly 70% of women's claims for asylum are rejected at the initial decision stage and that a high proportion of initial decisions on women's claims (up to 41%) were overturned at appeal in 2011. Muggeridge and Maman (2011) argue that the proportion of women's claims that go on to be overturned at appeal demonstrates problems with UKBA's initial decision making.

At the end of 2011, UKBA introduced additional changes to the asylum process in order to make it more gender-sensitive, the impact of which are yet to be assessed. These changes include the appointment of a women's champion and a trafficking champion (Querton, 2012:57) and the piloting of a mandatory one day training programme on gender issues for case owners (Dorling etc. 2012:27).

Home Office interviews

Two interviews are conducted by Home Office staff to assess an asylum-seeker's claim in relation to the five grounds of the refugee convention and also judge the credibility of their claim: the screening interview and the substantive interview.

The screening interview

Since July 2011 asylum seekers making in-country asylum claims must arrange an appointment for their screening interview at the Asylum Screening Unit in Croydon. The accessibility of the Asylum Screening Unit in Croydon has been questioned, especially for those women who have children, have to travel long distances or do not have the financial means to travel (Querton, 2012). The physical environment of the Asylum Screening Unit impacts upon women asylum seeker's experience of claiming asylum. Querton (2012:57) states, 'a lack of privacy…at the Asylum Screening Unit affects women asylum seekers' ability to put their claim forward in a fair manner'.

The substantive interview

Asylum-seeking women find the substantive interview with case owners to be both traumatic and confusing (Querton, 2012). For those who are victims of sexual violence, Home Office interviews can be particularly stressful and anxiety

The impact of gender and experiences of gender-related persecution

provoking (Bögner et al, 2007). According to a study by Bögner *et al.* (2007:80) those who had experienced sexual violence 'also described...greater difficulty in disclosure of personal information [such as an experience of sexual assault] during their Home Office interview'. A further study conducted by Bögner *et al.* (2009) found that some claimants' ability to disclose was impeded by the fact that the UKBA 'officials reminded them of police or officials from their home country' (ibid: 527) and made them feel 'persecuted' (ibid: 526). This study concludes that additional training for interviewing officials would be beneficial in order to facilitate a more positive experience for those disclosing sensitive information (ibid).

Individual asylum claims rest on the credibility of each asylum seeker's story and 'late disclosure, or description of incidents in later interviews of which no mention is made in the first, is commonly cited as a reason to doubt an asylum seeker's credibility'(Bogner *et al.*, 2007:80). Many asylum-seeking women do not disclose experiences of rape or other forms of sexual violence in either the screening interview or substantive interview and it has been suggested that this is 'a result of the failure of investigating personnel to attend to subtle cues, ask appropriately probing questions and create space for free-flowing dialogue' (Baillot, Cowan & Munro, 2012:292).

Same-gender interviewing officers and interpreters can have a positive effect upon an asylum-seekers' willingness to disclose experiences of sexual violence (Bögner *et al.*, 2009). Although female asylum-seekers are entitled to a female interviewing officer and evidence shows that all requests for this are complied with, many women do not state a preference for this due to a lack of understanding and not wanting to appear difficult (Muggeridge & Maman, 2011:35). Muggeridge and Maman (2011:35) report that only two (out of 39) of the women interviewed for their study had requested a female case owner and despite the plan for the New Asylum Model to provide each asylum seeker with a single case owner, most do not meet the same case owner more than once (ibid: 67). Muggeridge and Maman's (2011:66) reveal that questioning during the asylum interview was often inappropriate and 'demonstrated a lack of knowledge on the part of case owners regarding gender-related harm and persecution. It was also revealed that interviews are often long, psychological trauma was not considered by case owners and 'childcare was not consistently provided across regions' (ibid).

Detained Fast Track

Many asylum-seeking women are routed into the Detained Fast Track system (DFT). Home Office statistics (2009) reveal that since DFT for women was

The impact of gender and experiences of gender-related persecution

introduced in 2005, 2,055 women have been routed into it. A quarter of women interviewed for Dorling *et al's* (2012:15) study had been detained in the UK. The decision to route an asylum seeker into DFT is made during a screening interview. It is here that it is decided whether the claim is straightforward and capable of being decided quickly. However, it has been questioned how a claim can be deemed 'straightforward' when the immigration officers who conduct the screening interviews are not allowed to ask any questions regarding the substance of someone's claim (Cutler, 2007:18).

Time spent in detention has been studied in relation to levels of severe distress. A study into the mental health implications of detaining asylum seekers found that anxiety, depression, PTSD were commonly reported amongst detainees (Robjant, Hassan & Katona, 2009:306).

A report commissioned by Human Rights Watch entitled *Fast Tracked Unfairness* argues that DFT is unsuitable for complex cases such as gender-related claims for asylum (Van Gulik, 2010). This is echoed by Hobson *et al.* (2008a:42) who assert 'women's cases based on sexual violence are not properly presented under the fast-track system'. UKBA's own research concurs: 'The referral mechanism to the detained fast-track was not sufficiently robust to identify potential gender-related claims which are not suitable for fast track' (NAM Quality Team, 2006). Cutler's (2007:18) report argues that the 'Home Office's own policy on who should be in DFT is not followed in many cases'. Women rape and torture survivors, and women who do not meet the detention criteria are sent to Yarl's Wood [Immigration Removal Centre], including women who have explicitly said at their screening interview they are claiming asylum because of rape' (ibid:18). Furthermore, despite international guidelines, which recommend that people who have experienced extreme sexual violence should not be held in detention, the Refugee Council reports (2009:48) that 'trafficked women are routinely detained in the UK in immigration detention centres or prison.'

A report published by Bail for Immigration Detainees, detailing women's experiences of the detained fast track process, states that the swift process means that the women have 'no time to prepare their asylum case', that they 'do not have enough time with their lawyers', and then are 'detained for long periods once their case has been refused' (Cutler, 2007:3). As women's claims are often more complex, the limited time with legal representatives in DFT acerbates the difficulty of preparing a woman asylum seeker's case. In addition, legal aid in DFT is only guaranteed for the initial stage but not for appeals; 'one third of women who are refused at the initial stage in the Detained Fast Track are not granted legal

The impact of gender and experiences of gender-related persecution

representation at appeals because it is not deemed that the pass the legal aid merits test' (Cheikh Ali et al., 2012: 117).

Dispersal

As a consequence of the Immigration and Asylum Act 1999, asylum seekers requiring accommodation are dispersed to areas away from the Greater London area, until a decision regarding their asylum application has been reached (UKBA, 2009). Research conducted into the impact of dispersal on asylum seekers reveals that it 'fracture[s] the connection between refugees/asylum seekers and their well-established frameworks of community support and organisational structures [Refugee Community Organisations] previously available in London and the South East' (Zetter, Griffiths & Sigona, 2005:172). Despite this policy, many asylum seekers and refugees find their way to London. A study conducted by Robinson, Anderson & Musterd (2003) found that 1/5 of 56,000 asylum seekers had moved from dispersal regions to London whilst waiting for a decision from UKBA 'because of feelings of isolation from their community and/or harassment in the dispersal regions.'

It has been reported that the dispersal of asylum seekers with serious medical conditions, such as HIV/AIDS results in asylum seekers being 'forced to share accommodation with strangers with little regard for their privacy, hygiene or the sensitivity of their condition' (Refugee Council, 2005:24).

UK Border Agency accommodation

According to Dumper (2002a:11) 'since the dispersal system was introduced its inability to accommodate women asylum seekers adequately has been an area of great concern'. Dumper's report (2002a) investigates asylum-seeking women's sense of safety in their accommodation: 'Women have found themselves living in mixed-sex accommodation, sharing intimate living space with men from different cultures and nationalities' (ibid). Querton (2012:68) has also expressed unease about the provision of initial accommodation 'where men and women are placed in the same corridor and communal bathrooms have shower cubicles only closed by curtains' and where 'the gender ratio of staff in supported accommodation is not set out as a requirement in the specification of the contract between the UKBA and housing providers'. Querton's (2012:68) report for Asylum Aid, *I feel as a woman I'm not Welcome*, expresses 'concerns about housing officers entering unannounced into women's rooms' and even 'instances of sexual harassment in initial accommodation'. Despite special accommodation being available to victims of trafficking, it has been noted that this is often not made available in practice as

The impact of gender and experiences of gender-related persecution

'women are routed into initial accommodation without having had a choice even if there was disclosure of trafficking' (ibid:67). There are also concerns about the limited number of bed space in accommodation for victims of trafficking as well as 'some providers having conditions of entry such as cooperating with the police' (Cheikh Ali et al., 2012: 153).

It has been observed that newly arrived dispersed asylum seekers are often housed in deprived areas where housing is cheap. These areas display poverty, crime and community tensions (Carter & El-Hassan, 2003). In a recent press release, Refugee Council (2012b) questioned a UKBA announcement that they have awarded new contracts to security firms to provide accommodation for asylum seekers: 'We have consistently raised concerns in the past about the poor standard of accommodation provided for many asylum seekers, and the situation has the potential to deteriorate further with very large super regional contracts'. It is worrying that large companies with no previous experiences of working with this vulnerable group, and thus with little or no appreciation of the needs and experiences of asylum-seeking women, will be responsible for providing this essential welfare service. Last year the UK government 'cut 50% of the funding for providers of wraparound services in initial accommodation' (Cheikh Ali et al., 2012:152) and it has been argued that this will negatively impact upon the services these organisations are able to offer, particularly gender-related services (ibid).

Destitution

Due to a high refusal rate at the initial decision stage (Home Office, 2011b) destitution is a common experience for female asylum-seekers in the UK (British Red Cross, 2010:19). If an asylum seeker's claim is refused and they do not satisfy the conditions of Section 4 support,[5] all support is stopped and they are made homeless. Some are forcibly removed from the UK but many remain in the country because they are out of touch with the authorities. There are also thousands of asylum seekers who are refused protection here under the Refugee Convention but it is deemed too dangerous for the UK government to return them to their country of origin (Williams & Kaye, 2010). Asylum seekers left in this position are in limbo; 'destitute, prohibited from working and unable to safely return home' (Williams & Kaye, 2010:4). According to British Red Cross (2010:19) 'most refused asylum seekers feel safer being destitute and homeless in the UK than returning to their home country'. It was estimated that 283,500 refused asylum seekers were living in the UK in 2005 and 'this seems likely to have increased' (Crawley et al., 2011:5). British Red Cross (2010:18) state that the number of destitute asylum seekers

The impact of gender and experiences of gender-related persecution

accessing their services and relying on their food parcels is increasing: 'in 2004 we directly assisted 7,920 destitute asylum seekers and by 2009 this had increased to more than 11,600'. Research suggests that 'many asylum seekers have been destitute for more than six months and a significant proportion for more than two years' (Crawley, Hemmings & Price, 2011:5). Experiencing destitution for long periods of time is detrimental to health. Research by Refugee Action (2006:83) found that although 80% of the destitute asylum seekers in their sample were relatively young, between the ages of 21 and 40, 83% of those surveyed said that they had developed serious health problems since arriving in the UK.

Destitution and the asylum process

Destitution does not just occur upon refusal of an asylum claim. Research demonstrates that it can occur at many points during the asylum process (ibid). Delays in receiving Section 4 support and in accommodation becoming available have been reported (Williams & Kaye, 2010). A study in Leeds revealed that 'waiting for Section 4 to begin' was a cause of destitution for 33% of individuals' (British Red Cross, 2010:8). According to Refugee Council (2011:3), complications can prevent asylum seekers accessing the support they are entitled to: 'People can be refused asylum support for a variety of reasons which can include not applying in time, disagreements over whether a person is destitute and matters relating to the applicants' co-operation with UKBA'.

It is frequently argued that asylum seekers receive too little to live on and this leaves them dependent on hand-outs from charities and faith groups and on the generosity of friends (Williams & Kaye, 2010). Destitution is also reported to occur when asylum seekers are not aware of the support available to them or if they do not access state support because they are afraid of making contact with the authorities (Crawley, Hemmings & Price, 2011).

Destitute asylum seekers are able to apply to UKBA for housing and support and if this is refused they can appeal the decision to the asylum support tribunal. However, it has been observed that the number of 'women appellants attending hearings is consistently low' (Hickey, 2011:3). Numerous barriers have been described as an explanation for this gender imbalance, including health, childcare responsibilities, pregnancy and a lack of understanding of the process (ibid:5-6).

Homelessness

Those whose claims are refused become homeless, are forced to sleep rough, stay with friends or sleep in the accommodation of other asylum seekers (British Red

The impact of gender and experiences of gender-related persecution

Cross, 2010:21). Two thirds of the women interviewed by Dorling et al (2012:14) who were refused asylum had experienced destitution; they argue that female refused asylum seekers are at continued risk of sexual violence and exploitation due to their experiences of destitution. Of the 45 women interviewed, 7 had experienced sexual violence on the streets or where they were staying (ibid). This is corroborated by a Refugee Action report (2006), which found that 60% of participants had slept on the street on at least one occasion, with women often attracting unwanted attention, harassment and sexual abuse.

Homelessness occurs even if an asylum seeker is granted refugee status. A study into the homelessness sector in 2004 revealed that 'of the 2,431 bed spaces in 58 hostels undertaking a one night count, a fifth were occupied by refugees' (The London Housing Foundation, 2004:3). The study states that the majority of these were refugees rather than asylum seekers and that 60% 'had been resident in the UK for a long time before becoming resident at the hostels' and were 'homeless for reasons other than the asylum process' (ibid:6). Another 30% were homeless due to being asked to move on from NASS [now UKBA] accommodation once they have been granted asylum (ibid). The report demonstrates that a significant number of refugees experience homelessness at the end of the asylum process, but also that many continue to be vulnerable to homelessness even when they have been in the UK for several years (ibid). The study surveyed homeless residential services and hostels: 'Most agencies [surveyed] ... do not have specific policies about working with refugees and asylum seekers (ibid:9). It concludes that due to a lack of knowledge of working with this group 'Front line staff in the sector would benefit from more information to assist them in working effectively with refugees and asylum seekers' (ibid).

3.4 **Refugee women's vulnerability to sexual violence**

Refugee women's experiences of rape

Destitution exacerbates refugee women's vulnerability to sexual violence. Numerous studies have argued that not only do women experience gender-related violence prior to arriving in the UK, but they are also more vulnerable to sexual violence in the UK than the rest of the UK population (Refugee Council, 2009:32). The Refugee Council (2009:32) states that 'even when women have arrived in the UK they remain one of the groups that are a higher risk of rape'. They explain that refugee women are 'highly likely to belong to one or more of the groups that are at far higher risk of rape than the UK average of 5%: young women;

The impact of gender and experiences of gender-related persecution

poor women; women living in social housing; women in poor health and single, separated or divorced women' (ibid). Young refugee women are therefore at particular risk of experiencing rape or sexual assault. The vulnerability of young single women refugees and asylum seekers is exacerbated by the fact that they can 'find themselves living on their own in a strange town' and 'young women are particularly open to exploitation by the men around them and can become pregnant, adding further to their loneliness and vulnerability' (Dumper, 2004:30). In addition, once in the UK, destitute refugee women are more likely than men to be involved in commercial sex work and other forms of transactional relationships (Crawley et al., 2011).

Domestic violence

Research carried out by Phillimore et al. (2007:27) highlights 'Female refugees appeared to be more vulnerable to domestic violence in the UK, than in their home country'. A separation from wider family and social networks is offered as an explanation of this increased vulnerability (ibid). Women asylum seekers living in UKBA accommodation are able to access support and alternative UKBA accommodation as stated in the UKBA Policy Bulletin 70 (UK Border Agency, 2004). However it has been argued that it would be more appropriate to provide 'specialist refuge accommodation for domestic violence' (Querton, 2012:69) for these women as opposed to alternative UKBA accommodation.

Refugee women experiencing domestic violence in the UK face multiple barriers to leaving an abusive relationship. Those who are refused asylum and others who have an insecure immigration status, have been trafficked or overstayed their visa are not able to access any form of emergency accommodation including refuges for women who are victims of domestic violence (Amnesty International & Southall Black Sisters, 2008). The majority of these refuges only accept women who are eligible to claim housing benefit or income support. Amnesty International and Southall Black Sisters (2008:8) argue that 'all women require protection in order to escape violence against them. They need to be able to approach police and social services without fear of being left in the street, detained or removed to their country of origin – which can lead to other risks to their life or safety'.

For women claiming asylum as a dependent, their entitlement to welfare support and accommodation is subject to their partner's claim. As Dumper (2004:18) notes, if the relationship breaks down or the woman experiences abuse:

The impact of gender and experiences of gender-related persecution

'There is a risk that the application for asylum made by the husband for them both would be in jeopardy if a wife left her husband and made a claim in her own right...alternatively, it could mean that the woman is no longer seen as being dependent on her husband and therefore has no basis for staying in the UK.'

These barriers make it incredibly difficult for an asylum-seeking woman experiencing domestic violence in the UK to leave an abusive or violent relationship.

3.5 Accessing services and support

Mistrust of authorities

Refugees and asylum seekers of both sexes have been described as experiencing difficulties in accessing the services and support they need (Phillimore et al, 2007). Refused asylum seekers are often afraid of accessing support from voluntary organisations due to a fear that they are affiliated with the Home Office and they will be forced to return to their home country (Crawley et al., 2011). As Crawley *et al.* (2011:25) state 'refused asylum seekers have an almost universal fear of interaction with the state and its representatives, and are extremely unlikely to access state resources for fear that this may result in deportation'. For instance, research shows that many women asylum seekers fear the appeals process because of 'negative experiences of authority in countries of origin' (Hickey, 2011:6).

It is not just refused asylum seekers that experience a mistrust of authority. Those who are in the process of going through the asylum process are also reported to be reluctant to use health services for fear that it would negatively affect their claim for asylum (Kanani, Webster, Ndegwa, Murphy, & Stevens, 2001). Phillimore *et al's* (2007:18) study found that 'The trauma of their experiences going through the asylum system led to several participants feeling very suspicious of authorities in general. This meant GPs, housing officers and Jobcentre Plus officers'.

Awareness of support available

Whilst both refugee men and women experience difficulties accessing services and support, it has been found that women face added barriers. A study into refugee well-being and mental health explains that 'in the absence of social networks and restricted access to ESOL women are less likely to know where to seek help and

The impact of gender and experiences of gender-related persecution

advice about how to access services' (Phillimore et al., 2007:26). The difficulties refugee women face in accessing services are related to a number of factors including: 'having nowhere to go for advice or receiving incorrect advice from peers, inability to communicate, and not knowing about their rights and entitlements' (ibid:23).

Impact of gender roles on access to services

Cultural expectations of a woman's role as a wife and a mother is another barrier to accessing services. Childcare responsibilities along with expectations that women will take care of the home mean that women are restricted in their movement more than men (Phillimore et al., 2007:26). Childcare responsibilities, for instance, can be a barrier to submitting an appeal as they make it 'difficult to travel to an agency for advice, let alone travel to London for the hearing' and women often do not want 'to bring the children to the tribunal as it has no childcare facilities' (Hickey, 2011:5).

Access to healthcare

All refugee and asylum seekers can register with a GP and receive free NHS hospital treatment. However, access to healthcare differs for refused asylum seekers. In England refused asylum seekers who are receiving Section 4 or Section 95[5] support from UKBA are entitled to free NHS hospital treatment. Refused asylum seekers who are not in receipt of the above support are not entitled to free hospital treatment but are still entitled to free primary care services. Nevertheless, hospitals are obliged to provide treatment which is deemed 'urgent', which includes maternity treatment, antenatal care and treatment to prevent a condition becoming life threatening. According to the British Medical Association (2012) 'GP practices retain the discretion to register refused asylum seekers to the same extent that they have the discretion in relation to registering any patient, regardless of his or her residency status'.

Access to GP services

Manal's (1996) study of asylum-seeking women in Brighton, 82% of the women interviewed were dissatisfied with their GP, largely due to the inaccessibility of the service.

Whilst, another study of asylum seekers and refugees and their experiences of primary health care established that 'those refugees without support from friends, family and refugee agencies may have the most difficulty accessing GPs', concluding that 'the problem of poor access for those with inadequate support may be improved by better education and support for GPs in how to provide for refugees.' (Bhatia & Wallace, 2007).

Dumper (2004:22-23) explains how women refugees experience additional barriers to accessing healthcare: 'They may be restricted by cultural codes from leaving the house without a male chaperone, they may not know enough English to use public transport, they may not be used to using public transport, and they may be caring for children and family members which restricts their movement. In addition they may be forbidden to attend any place where men gather'. Cultural barriers are also cited by Taylor (2009) who claims that women refugees are 'more likely to report poor health and depression, yet in some cultures may be dependent on a man to disclose this'. Access to GP services is also difficult for those who are homeless or living in very temporary accommodation (Aspinall & Watters, 2010:20). It has been reported that barriers to accessing GP services has resulted in asylum seekers and refugees relying on accident and emergency services, which causes 'increasing healthcare costs and pressure on A and E services' (ibid). In addition, a Home Office report found that the dispersal process meant that asylum seekers were being 'moved from place to place', which makes it 'difficult to obtain registration with medical practitioners and healthcare programmes' (Johnson, 2003:2).

Language barriers

According to Burnett and Peel (2001) language and the ability to express health needs is the main difficulty refugee and asylum seekers face when accessing health services. Language barriers result in difficulties registering and making an appointment (Aspinall &Watters, 2010:20). In Dumper's (2002a:15) study, 84% of refugee women interviewed said that they always or sometimes need an interpreter however only 52% had access to an interpreter when visiting the doctor. Mind (2009:3) argues that there is also a 'lack of knowledge among mainstream healthcare professionals of how to work with interpreters' and 'many GP practices do not provide interpreting services'. Bhatia and Wallace (2007) state, 'professional interpreters may not always be desired and that instead, it may be advisable to reach a consensus as to who should be used as an interpreter'. They go on to describe how many participants in their study stated that they 'much preferred the using of family and friends as interpreters' and one of the reasons given for this was that 'they did not trust the interpreter' (ibid). Those participants who did not trust interpreters were from Somalia and 'cited inter-communal violence in their country of origin as a reason' (ibid).

The impact of gender and experiences of gender-related persecution

Access to healthcare for victims of gender-related violence

In a study conducted by Refugee Council (2005:17), 64% of victims of torture and/or rape mentioned counselling as one of their unmet needs. This study revealed that many (34%) 'had not declared this need to NASS [now UKBA] because they felt shame or stigma or feared being disbelieved, or simply because they had not been asked to' (ibid). A delay in waiting times, dispersal and delays due to the need for interpreters were given as reasons for the lack of counselling provision for this group (ibid). Furthermore, Querton (2012:71) reveals that 'there are no psychotherapeutic interventions for this group' in initial accommodation. Asylum seekers with mental health problems are referred to a specialist by their GP, however, access to this service can be complicated as a result of dispersal (ibid).

Refugee women who have experienced sexual violence are found to be 'reluctant to speak to white male GPs about their experiences' (Phillimore et al., 2007:26). The availability of sexual violence services is limited and it has been reported that less than one in ten of local authorities have specialised services that would cater to the needs of women who have experienced gender-related persecution (Coy, Lovett & Kelly, 2008).

Those women whose asylum claims are refused are not eligible for free secondary health care and this 'risks denying vital health care to the most vulnerable of the vulnerable: survivors of sexual violence who have been rendered destitute and homeless' (Refugee Council, 2009:53).

Amnesty International and Southall Black Sisters have criticised the provision of support for women with insecure immigration statuses who are victims of domestic violence in the UK. They argue that 'Local authorities take the view that they have no obligation to provide for women subject to the 'no recourse to public funds requirement' when in fact the woman may be eligible for assistance because the woman has children and/or specific needs for care and attention (Amnesty International & Southall Black Sisters, 2008:12). Their report, *No recourse, no safety,* Amnesty International and Southall Black Sisters (2008:13) reveals that despite local authorities undertaking eligibility tests and assessments of need on for women fleeing domestic violence, 'the majority...will rule that women in these situations are not eligible for support'.

Maternal Health outcomes

In the UK, the maternal health outcomes for asylum-seeking women are extremely poor (Beecher Bryant (2011:3). It has been argued that this is because the financial support pregnant asylum-seeking women are eligible for in the UK is 'significantly

The impact of gender and experiences of gender-related persecution

lower than for mainstream welfare benefits' and as a result they end up living in poverty (Cheikh Ali et al., 2012: 154).

Cultural differences appear to be the most common barrier in regards to access to maternity care. Beecher Bryant's (2011:10) study for Maternity Action states that 'some women were not familiar with the role of the midwife'. Midwives interviewed in this study claimed that some pregnant asylum seekers may be 'unfamiliar with the idea of seeking antenatal care and this was not available in their home country' (ibid). The report asserts that there are very few midwives specialising in caring for refugee and asylum-seeking women in the UK (ibid). Lack of money for transport and dispersal to another area of the UK were mentioned as barriers to continuity of care (ibid). Maternity Action are currently delivering a training programme for midwives on the needs of refugee women in response to the maternal health outcomes amongst refugee women (ibid).

Access to legal services

There is growing concern about the lack of legal aid solicitors offering asylum and immigration advice. Evidence indicates that there is a shortage of legal representatives for asylum-seeking women outside of London, particularly in Leeds and Cardiff: 'women in Leeds and Cardiff were often represented by solicitors based in London' (Muggeridge & Maman, 2011:42). It has been noted that 'the dispersal of asylum seekers to various parts of the UK can impact their case because they are unable to locate quality advisors in the area that they are dispersed to and their representation is interrupted' (Hobson, Cox, & Sagovsky, 2008b:21). According to Muggeridge and Maman (2011:43) 'Cuts in legal aid, the decline in private solicitors firms offering asylum and immigration advice and the closure of Refugee and Migrant Justice...are likely to lead to an increase in unrepresented asylum seekers, particularly at appeal'.

The funding framework for legal aid means that legal representatives are not paid for the work required before taking an asylum seeker's case to appeal (Muggeridge & Maman, 2011). This often discourages solicitors from 'taking the most complex cases to appeal' and can result in women asylum seekers (whose cases are typically more complex) going to appeal without legal representation (ibid:7). The situation is most fraught in 'Cardiff, where half of the women who went to appeal did so without any legal representation' (ibid).

Access to legal support for those in DFT is particularly difficult. Unlike in the UK criminal justice system, women detainees at Yarl's Wood are 'frequently seen by male legal representatives' (Asylum Aid, 2007:2). Asylum Aid (2007:2) argues that women

The impact of gender and experiences of gender-related persecution

asylum seekers in detention should be 'represented by female legal representatives' and that the Legal Services Commission should ensure it 'is complying with the new Gender Equality Duty'. Querton (2012) outlines numerous difficulties that female asylum seekers faced when accessing legal representation, including that, many solicitors 'only made appointments with them after they had attended their substantive asylum interview and thus did not frontload cases' (ibid: 61). Some of the women interviewed for the study revealed that their solicitors decided not to continue to represent them after UKBA's initial decision and others 'were not always informed that they could appeal the decision by their solicitor to refuse them legal aid'(ibid). This results in 'many women asylum seekers going through the asylum process without adequate representation and thus could only later maker further submissions on the basis of evidence that could have been submitted earlier' (ibid).

Furthermore, it has been argued that although the *Legal Aid, Sentencing and Punishment of Offenders Act* will not directly affect legal aid funding for asylum cases it will result in 'many law firms being unable to continue their immigration and asylum work' because it will no longer be possible to 'cross-subsidise' the costs with 'less complex immigration work' (Dorling et al, 2012:26).

Access to education and employment

Low levels of English language ability have been identified as a major factor in preventing educational attainment for refugee and asylum seekers of both genders. A study conducted by Bloch (2002a) for the Department for Work and Pensions established that a high proportion of refugees and asylum seekers do not complete their ESOL language courses. The main reasons being childcare and family commitments; factors which disproportionately affect women (ibid).

Refugee women's educational background can vary considerably. A study of the Somali community found that only 3% of Somali women held qualifications prior to their arrival compared with a 25% of men (Carter, 2003:26). Conversely, with 68% of the refugee women surveyed for a study in 2002 educated to university level in their country of origin, many refugee women find themselves over qualified and unable to find work to match their qualifications (Dumper, 2002b). A barrier faced by all refugees seeking to continue their education and enter the job market in the UK is that of a lack of recognition of the qualifications gained in their country of origin (Arai, 2005).

Refugee women and unemployment

It has been claimed that employment is central to successful refugee integration (Bloch, 2002b). It is illegal for asylum seekers to work whilst they are waiting for their

The impact of gender and experiences of gender-related persecution

claim to be processed by UKBA, however some do work illegally in order to survive (Crawley *et al.*, 2011). Even those with refugee status and therefore entitled to work experience high unemployment; 29% of refugees surveyed by Bloch (2002a:3) were working, compared with 60% of the ethnic minority population. In Bloch's (2002a:124) research, men were more likely to be employed than women, with only 15% of women being in paid employment compared to 43% of men. Refugee women have also been found to be 'suffering greater work exclusion where they have entered the UK as dependents on their husband's asylum claim (Carter, 2003:30). Reasons cited for this include lack of childcare support from family and friends and a lack of professional networks in comparison to men (Dumper, 2002b). It has been seen that unemployed refugees 'had low levels of knowledge about statutory provision' and 'just under half (49%) had heard of any schemes run by Jobcentre Plus' (Dumper, 2002b:3).

Those refugees who do find work are often under-employed: 'many refugees with higher skills and/or professional qualifications are only able to find out at levels below their skills and are therefore underemployed' (Carter, 2003:27). Research on refugee employment revealed that, of those that are employed, the majority work in catering and hospitality, interpreting, retail, cleaning, security, factor, administrative and clerical jobs' (Bloch, 2002a).

3.6 Summary of the extant literature & current knowledge

Many refugee women in the UK will have experienced gender-related persecution either in their country of origin or the UK. However there is reported to be a lack of specialist service provision for women who have experienced persecution of this nature.

Refugees of both sexes experience additional health problems to the rest of the UK population. For refugee women who have experienced sexual violence, these health problems are compounded by the physical and mental health consequences of gender-related forms of persecution.

Women refugees are more likely than their male counterparts to suffer from PTSD, depression and anxiety. Experiences in their country of origin, the asylum process and adjusting to life in the UK all contribute to and/or acerbate mental health problems among refugee women. However, research indicates that counselling is an unmet need amongst this group.

For those who are victims of sexual violence, Home Office interviews can be particularly traumatic and confusing as they experience greater difficulty

The impact of gender and experiences of gender-related persecution

disclosing personal information and this can affect the credibility of their asylum claim.

Although it is a widely held view that Detained Fast Track (DFT) is not suitable for gender-related claims for asylum, asylum-seeking women continue to be detained in the UK, including those who have been raped or trafficked into the country. The experience of being detained further contributes to their trauma and distress. Access to legal support for those in DFT is particularly difficult and women detainees are often seen by male legal representatives.

Although developments in case law have demonstrated that it is accepted that there are particular forms of persecution that are gender-specific, the asylum process continues to be biased against women's claims for asylum. Despite the implementation of UKBA's instruction for case workers, Gender Issues in the Asylum Claim, these guidelines are not being fully observed by UKBA staff and this has resulted in a high proportion of women's claims for asylum being rejected at the initial decision stage.

It is reported that the provision of initial accommodation for asylum-seeking women is inadequate and not sensitive to their needs and experiences as women. This situation may be set to worsen with the announcement from UKBA of new contracts to security firms to provide accommodation for asylum seekers. This will result in companies with no experience of working with this vulnerable group, and therefore little appreciation of their experiences and needs, providing an essential welfare service to these individuals.

Many refugee women experience destitution in the UK. Those whose claims are refused or experience destitution as a result of the asylum process are at continued risk of sexual violence due to their vulnerability to homelessness, transactional relationships and exploitation. As a result of their poverty, poor accommodation, poor health and lack of support structure refugee women are likely to belong to one of the groups at a higher risk of rape or sexual violence. These women are also more vulnerable to domestic violence in the UK than in their home country and often face multiple barriers to leaving an abusive relationship.

Refugee women experience more difficulties accessing services and support than their male counterparts, this is often a result of their role as a mother, cultural practices, and their responsibilities in the home. Difficulties accessing services and support are also related to a lack of awareness of the help available, lack of money for transport, having nowhere to go for advice, an inability to communicate in English, poor provision and understanding of how to use interpreters and the absence of social networks.

The impact of gender and experiences of gender-related persecution

Dispersal also appears to have a negative impact upon asylum-seeking women's access to services; it results in a lack of continuity of care in maternity service provision, disrupts counselling and mental health provision, results in little or no access to legal representation and affects access to GP services.

Notes

4 Gender-specific persecution refers to forms persecution, which may be carried out for reasons unrelated to gender, for instance 'raped because of holding a particular political opinion' (UK Border Agency, 2010:5)

5 Section 4 support is a form of short-term support for refused asylum seekers 'who are destitute and unable to leave the UK immediately due to circumstances beyond their control' (UK Border Agency (n.d), *Section 4 Support*)

6 Section 95 is a form of support for asylum seekers who are deemed to be 'destitute' and who have applied for asylum as soon as reasonably practicable'. This support takes the form of smaller scale accommodation and a low level of financial support (UK Border Agency (n.d), *Assessing Destitution*).

The impact of gender and experiences of gender-related persecution

© IARS

Refugee and asylum seeking women's experiences of health services in Greater London: Findings from the fieldwork

4.1 Introduction

This chapter focusses on refugee and asylum seeking women's experiences of GP (General Practitioner) services in light of the multiple disadvantages they face as a result of experiences of gender-related violence and their immigration status. In the pursuit of an equal society, it is vital to ensure that all individuals receive equality of opportunity to access public services as well as achieving equality of outcome for vulnerable groups, who have a particular set of complex needs. This chapter addresses the problems that refugee women face in achieving both equality of opportunity and equality of outcome with GP services.

The chapter thematically explores the problems that refugee women face with this service including the registration process and challenges for those women who do not have a permanent address or who have to move house frequently. The significance of establishing a relationship with *one* GP for refugee women will be addressed. Insight is also provided into the experience of those women with low levels of English language ability and the impact of using formal and informal interpreters on their experience of GP services.

4.2 Accessing health services

This section explores refugee women's experiences of accessing GP services. Participants were asked to describe their experiences of registering with a GP practice and answers varied considerably, with some experiencing no problems in this area and others who had been unable to register at all.

Almost half of the asylum-seeking women who participated in the study outlined difficulties with registering with a GP practice because they had been unable to provide the documentation some practices require to register new patients:

I went to one of the practices when I was in bad condition, they didn't help me, they said we can't register you because, it's like, 'you've got no status'. They

Experiences of GP services in Greater London

just started asking me for papers, passport and everything, which I didn't have and proof of address. So I tried to tell them, I don't have all the things you are talking about but I'm here for help because I'm sick. So what they did, they told me that they can't help me unless I go back home and I bring the things they need so that they can register me (DM01)

She [the receptionist] told me if you don't have two proofs of address then we cannot register you...So I told her, I'm not allowed to work so I don't have proofs of bills, the only things I have are letters from the Home Office and my ID card' (PM01)

Both of these women were asked by reception staff to provide forms of identification, such as proof of address documentation and passports, that, as asylum-seekers, they were not able to provide. PM01 related how she had also experienced problems registering with another GP practice because she had been unable to provide an NHS number or any previous medical records:

She [receptionist] said you need to have your previous doctor card and I said I don't have it I've never had a doctor and she said there's no way you could be in this country and never had a doctor. And I said yes, I've been seen by a doctor in detention that's the only time I've been seen by a doctor (PM01)

This participant, who at the time of interview had still been unable to register with a GP, reported being asked by a receptionist for her 'previous doctor card', which she was unable to provide because the only time she had been seen by a GP in the UK 'was in detention'. She told us that whilst she had been in detention a doctor had informed her that she needed to have a cervical smear scan and since leaving detention she had attempted to register with a doctor in order to access this medical treatment.

This woman's difficulty with registering with another GP practice was further complicated by a receptionist's lack of understanding of asylum-seekers' entitlements to primary health care:

Yesterday...it's the lady that came to ask for my visa I said I don't have my passport and she said no we need to see your visa. They said we cannot register you we have to see your visa...I felt so bad I felt like I was at the airport being asked for a visa' (PM01)

Experiences of GP services in Greater London

The receptionist's request to see her visa suggests a lack of understanding of the situation of asylum-seekers and their entitlements to primary health care in the UK.

The challenges this woman faced with registering with a GP practice and her increasing anxiety about her physical health contributed to her worsening depression:

> *Yesterday [after trying to register with a surgery near where she is living] I felt so down, I just walked home and I called my friend and I said I'm not going to try again (PM01)*

She described the experience as making her feel 'down' and hopeless about being able to register with a GP.

Some participants reported that difficulties with registering with GP practices had caused delays to their access to health care as they had had to search for a surgery that would register them. One woman reported not having a GP for three years until the British Red Cross helped her to find one that would register her:

> *I was three years without a GP before and then British Red Cross found me one – the one I'm with now' (KC01)*

Another woman spoke of being unable to register with one GP practice, but eventually was able to register elsewhere:

> *They refused to register me because I couldn't provide proof of address. So I went elsewhere and they registered me' (KC02)*

Several other participants, who had been able to register with GP practices, had done so with the help of specialist refugee charities:

> *I saw [refugee charity] in the newspaper...and then they printed out a list of practices in my area' (DM01)*

> *Because I'm an asylum seeker and don't have a passport or anything like that so I had to go to [refugee charity] and they wrote a letter to the GP and then the GP accepted me but before they didn't (HYM01)*

Experiences of GP services in Greater London

In these instances refugee charities, who had provided advice and advocacy support on behalf of these women, were crucial to enabling these women to access GP services.

The impact of a transient lifestyle on access to GP services

When asked about their experiences of accessing GP services, many refugee women depicted the difficulties associated with living a very transient lifestyle, either as a result of being moved around by UKBA or because they have no permanent address and have to rely on friends and family to provide them with a place to stay. Both homelessness and regularly moving around London caused significant difficulties in relation to the participants' access to primary health services.

Regularly moving address compounds the difficulties refugee women face when accessing GP services as it requires them to register with a new GP practice every time they move. Due to the difficulties that many participants had experienced with registering with a GP when they first arrived in the UK, some reported choosing to stay with the same GP practice when they moved area, often meaning that they had to travel long distances for appointments:

> *I try not to change GPs because they will ask for this and for that and since I haven't got papers now I just want to keep it low key and not have like… so I'm sticking with the old GP so every time I have to go there (DN02)*

> *My problem is that I'm always moving from place to place. Now I'm in Wembley and I've been saying that I live in Camden. I've no fixed address. I've been travelling from Wembley to Camden to see my GP (FY13)*

> *I have to travel a long way to doctor's appointments, which takes a lot of time and money and I often miss appointments (WC02)*

Those who stated they had attempted to register with a GP practice in their new area recalled the problems they had experienced with this process. One woman explained that the challenges she faced with registering with a new practice meant that her healthcare was interrupted:

> *When I had my second child we changed areas so to go the new GP to register it was a little bit hard because I didn't have any paper work with me to show I*

Experiences of GP services in Greater London

was living at this address so they couldn't register me straight away. It took six months for me to see the doctor and repeat my prescription, like I was saying in the beginning; I had a lot of female problem. So waiting to be registered for that long was really really hard (OD03)

The delay with registering with a new GP practice affected this woman's access to prescriptions. This participant, who disclosed that she experienced gynaecological health problems as a result of being raped, found the experience of waiting to be registered for a long time particularly distressing.

Those with no permanent address experienced problems with accessing GP services. Five participants were homeless and spoke of living between a number of addresses and relying on the support of friends for a place to live. For one woman, this caused problems with her correspondence with her GP practice:

The problem is this, because sometimes I don't have a permanent place to stay right you have to change addresses. One month I'll be living one place, another...places to places. So when they send you a letter, they don't get you there, they send the letter back to the surgery and they'll be telling you 'no, we're cancelling you because your mail has been sent back...so it's not your fault because you don't have permanent place to stay. So you'll try to explain but you have to register with the GP where you are, where to register, that's a problem. Sometimes you get the letters, sometimes you don't. You might have 7,8 addresses, 8 friends to live with (FY04)

She described how as a consequence of moving from place to place and not receiving letters from her GP, the GP practice removed her from the patient register. From this account it appears that communication via post is problematic for those refugee women with a lack of a permanent address or who have to move regularly.

Summary

Asylum-seeking women (in contrast to those who have been granted Leave to Remain of Refugee Status) experience difficulties with registering with GP services as a result of some GP practices refusing to register new patients who are unable to provide proof-of-address documentation, as well as a lack of understanding on behalf of some reception staff of asylum-seekers' entitlements to primary health care. The experiences of the sample reflect the differences in practice between

Experiences of GP services in Greater London

different GP practices regarding the registration of asylum-seeking patients as a result of practices having the discretion to register any patient regardless of their immigration status (British Medical Association, 2012). Difficulties in finding a GP practice that will register them can delay an asylum-seeking woman's access to primary health care, something which is particularly distressing for those with pressing mental and physical health conditions.

Those refugee women who are homeless or who move areas frequently also experience problems with registering and communicating via post with GP services. This finding is supported by previous studies reporting the problems with accessing GP services for those asylum seekers who are homeless or living in temporary accommodation (Aspinall & Watters, 2010) and those who are moved from place to place as part of the dispersal process (Johnson, 2003).

To avoid the difficulties associated with registering with a new GP, some refugee women choose to remain with their original GP practice, often resulting in them travelling long distances for appointments. The difficulties refugee women experience in trusting professionals and the problems associated with disclosure and retelling their personal story also explains why some refugee women choose to remain with the same GP despite moving areas.

4.3 Building a relationship with one GP

Forming a trusting relationship with one GP was detailed by the research participants as crucial to a positive experience of GP services because of the challenges they face in trusting and disclosing sensitive personal information to professionals. Refugee women spoke of the difficulties they experienced in building trusting relationships with one GP, often because of being unable to see the same doctor each time they made an appointment and also because of having to change GP practice regularly as a result of moving area.

Many of the refugee women spoken to claimed that they often have to see several different doctors at the same GP practice and this made it challenging to build a relationship where disclosure of sensitive information was possible:

> *The first GP – I can talk to if she knows about me – I can tell everything private to her but when I go to 5 different GPs, I can't tell everything to everyone* (HYN01)

Another participant reported that she had never met the GP that she was supposed to be registered with and so was not sure who she could confide in:

Experiences of GP services in Greater London

> *I don't know my GP. I know them on paper but I don't know him – he is never available (inaudible) I don't know which one I can open up to'* (HYM01)

One woman discussed the reasons why she preferred to be seen by the same GP and found it hard to be seen by different doctors who were unfamiliar with her history:

> *I always want my GP to know more about my life I always want him to pay much attention on me, whenever I go there I want him to be the person I talk to* (DM01)

Building a relationship with one GP was reported to be particularly difficult for asylum-seeking women who move house frequently or who are homeless:

> *When you move again to another borough, it's really really hard to re-adjust because you've established a relationship with your GP* (OD02)

> *It was difficult to build a new relationship and I think we all prefer to see one person [GP] all the time because you end up having friendship with those people and now it's easy to communicate with them because they know you'* (FY04)

OD02 recounted the experience of changing GP practice as a result of moving house as 'really really hard to re-adjust' because it interrupted an 'established' relationship with her GP. Likewise, FY04 explained that 'friendships' are formed with GPs and that these established relationships make it 'easy to communicate' because the GP has an increased knowledge of their situation.

Establishing a relationship with a new GP was described as problematic for some refugee women because of the difficulty of re-telling their story and being asked questions about topics that can be difficult to discuss:

> *They've [other GPs] got all the information on the computer but they still feel they want to ask you [questions about your situation] and it's not easy* (FY01)

> *It's hard to communicate with that new doctor because they will be asking maybe one thing 10 times so you get annoyed with that'* (FY01)

Experiences of GP services in Greater London

> *It's very difficult to continually answer the same questions and retell the same problems (WC02)*

> *I mean I have an NHS number but they still ask me questions which remind me of my past (KC02)*

FY01 expressed frustration at being repeatedly asked the same questions by a new doctor familiarising themselves with her case. Likewise WC02 spoke of the challenge of 'retell[ing] the same problems' to different doctors. For KC02 moving to a new GP practice meant that she was asked questions that 'remind me of my past'.

Three participants expressed a preference for doctors to use their medical history information and NHS number to gain the information they needed about their condition rather than asking them questions, which they often found distressing. One woman preferred knowing that a doctor had access to her personal history on the computer system:

> *The thing is, for me, like when you go there sometimes they read your history on the system and they acquaint themselves with your problem so I've not really had a problem...they can check, this person that is coming to see me, what major things are many problems I've had. Even though I'm going there on a particular day with a particular problem but they've had a bit of my history (FY02)*

She commented that being seen by different GPs was not a problem for her because they were able to read her history 'on the system' and 'acquaint themselves' with her experiences.

Summary

Research participants placed particular emphasis on the importance of developing a trusting relationship with *one* GP who they can confide in. Developing a relationship with one doctor is important for refugee women so that they can be seen by someone who has a good understanding of their personal history, making it easier for them to communicate their needs. A sound awareness and sensitivity to their wider support needs increases the degree to which professionals are able to empathise with this vulnerable group, which in turn builds trust and aids disclosure.

The difficulties associated with being seen by different GPs for this group of women are having to repeatedly re-tell their personal stories and being asked questions that remind them of their past.

4.4 Problems associated with language, culture and communication

Of the refugee women interviewed, 75% rated their English language ability when they first arrived in the UK as 'Very little' or 'Not at all'. Twenty one interviews were conducted using interpreters, 45% of the sample. Those women who required an interpreter to participate in an interview for this study included six women who had been in the UK for ten years or more, indicating that low levels of English language is a significant problem for refugee women regardless of the length of time they have been in the UK.

Participants were asked whether they had experienced any difficulties associated with language when accessing GP services. One woman from Turkey who had been in the UK for nine years spoke about the difficulties she had trying to explain her health problems to her GP:

> *Because I'm having difficulties giving all the details, I can say a couple of words but I cannot give them the whole story. And also when they prescribe medication, all the information is in English and I don't know what I'm using' (IN01)*

A low level of English meant that this participant did not understand the medication that she had been prescribed by her GP. Her difficulties with English affected her ability to express herself fully and so was not able to provide her GP with 'the whole story'.

Another woman from Eritrea who did not speak any English when she first arrived in this country recounted a time when she had felt she had been discriminated against because of her lack of English:

> *I went to the hospital several times three years ago as my husband was ill but they kept turning me away. I think this was because of my English skills. It took four different visits to the emergency services to be taken seriously...Some nurses walk away when someone with poor language skills speaks to them, they should try harder to understand them and help (WC01)*

This participant felt that her low language skills had meant that she had not been given the attention she needed and that she had not been taken seriously by health professionals.

Experiences of GP services in Greater London

Experiences of using interpreters

Participants were asked whether they had used an interpreter whilst accessing GP services and were asked to explain the impact of this on their experience of the service. Twenty of the women interviewed said that they had used interpreters whilst accessing GP services:

At our GP surgery, every Wednesday and Thursday, interpreters are coming (IN05)

We use phone interpreters (IN04)

Yes, it was very good…it's easier to get points across (WC02)

Nine participants shared difficulties they had encountered as a result of using interpreters:

Sometimes it's a problem – sometime they are not translating exactly – some say you say 'A' but you said 'O' – you say no I didn't say that, it's not like that – it's not correct (HYM01)

So you say many word but they give only one word to the doctor' (IN04)

It was difficult for me to communicate with the GP when I first arrived because my English was basic. Interpreters didn't always explain things to the GP the way I wanted them to though (LH02)

These women all expressed concern that they had not been translated correctly by interpreters. Another participant explained that she preferred to not use an interpreter because of her concern about the accuracy of the interpreting:

It is frustrating when you cannot explain things yourself, you worry that the interpreter is not explaining things the way you want them to. I prefer not to use an interpreter (LH02)

LH02 found the experience of using an interpreter 'frustrating' as she was worried that the interpreter was not explaining things the way she wanted them to. It is difficult to know how these participants would have known whether they had

Experiences of GP services in Greater London

been translated correctly because of their low levels of English language. In some cases, participants had basic English, but were not able to communicate fluently and so may have been able to assess the quality of the interpreting to some degree. However, what appears to underlie their concern around using interpreters is a general lack of trust in interpreters to given an accurate translation. This relates to the difficulties refugee women experience in building trust professionals and those in professional more generally to be discussed in Chapter six.

When asked about their experiences of using interpreters, six of the women interviewed said that they had taken their children to GP appointments to interpret for them:

I take my daughter and my son when I go to the doctor (CN01)

Three participants reported that their GP had asked them to bring their children to interpret for them. Whilst some did not have a problem with this, for others it caused difficulties:

They tell me to bring my children to help me translate but I can't say everything in front of my children. I went once with my eldest daughter but she wasn't able to explain everything and it was embarrassing (IN01)

From this account, it seems that using children as informal interpreters for GP appointments can prevent an open dialogue between refugee women and their GPs because there may be some things that they might not want to disclose in front of their children. This participant, who had very basic English and struggled to express herself during our interview with her, recalled being told her GP to find someone who could interpret on her behalf:

They [GP] just told me just come with someone who have speak English. But who'll give me [interpret for me], my children are working, they are very busy in this country' (CN03)

With her children 'busy', it was difficult for her to find an informal interpreter to accompany her to see the GP. Communication stye?

Experiences of GP services in Greater London

Summary

Those research participants with low levels of English experienced problems with GP services as they were unable to fully express themselves or comprehend the nature of the medication they had been prescribed. Previous studies have shown that language and the ability to express health needs is the main difficulty refugee and asylum-seekers face when accessing health services (Burnett & Peel, 2001). Difficulties associated with language relate to the need for refugee women to have more time with their GP during appointments, especially when viewed in relation to the time it takes for these women to trust professionals and to disclose their personal story.

Whilst some of the women who participated in this study reported positive experiences of using interpreters during GP appointments, some expressed dissatisfaction over the quality of the interpreting and concern that their meaning had not been properly communicated to the GP. Difficulties were also detailed as a result of some GPs' encouragement of the use of informal interpreters, such as family members, as this proved problematic for those who had no family or support network in the UK. Using children to interpret was also sometimes described as problematic as it can hinder open communication with GPs on sensitive topics. This may act as a further obstacle to disclosure for refugee women, who already face multiple barriers to confiding their personal story to GPs. In contrast, a study conducted by Bhatia and Wallace (2007) found that participants preferred to use informal interpreters, such as family and friends, because of a lack of trust in interpreters as a result of inter-communal violence in their country of origin.

Refugee women's experiences of legal services in Greater London: Findings from the fieldwork

5.1 Introduction

This chapter examines research participants' experiences of accessing solicitor services and the impact of detention and dispersal on their experience of this service. The prevalence of refugee women paying for legal help is discussed as well as the problems they face in communicating with solicitors about the progress of asylum claims and the impact of children's presence during solicitor appointments.

5.2 Finding a solicitor

This section explores refugee women's experiences of accessing solicitor services and difficulties experienced by those who lacked understanding of legal aid and how the UK legal system operated.

Several participants expressed a lack of awareness of the role of solicitors when they first arrived in this country:

When I first came here, I didn't even know about solicitors (KC02)

If there is any way that they can let people know at Lunar House that you need a solicitor and to say that all the solicitors that you've got right to legal aid. So if you'd known this before I would save my money and go for legal aid and the solicitor would direct me properly and would tell me what to do and the first steps or what to do next (OT03)

OT03's experience was relatively common amongst participants in this study. 20% said that they had paid for a solicitor services due to a lack of awareness of their eligibility for legal aid. The majority of these women had paid for a solicitor for their initial claim and had then gone on to access legal aid to submit an appeal or a fresh claim for asylum, indicating that there is a lack of information provided on legal aid at the start of the asylum process.

Experiences of legal services in Greater London

All but one of those who reported paying for a solicitor had been referred by a friend:

Through my friend (LH02)

My friend recommended it. My family friend recommended (FY09)

I was referred through a friend (FY04)

He's from my country and he's been helping people before, a lot of people went to him. When my friend introduced me to him they said this man is helpful but err he's a paying man, you've got to pay, it's not a free solicitor' (FY04)

The first solicitor that I had I was referred by a friend (FY02)

I was directed by some friends to a solicitor (KC02)

A friend told me that I need a lawyer so I just look for one in the paper ... so I went to see a private lawyer which took me nearly £2000 after my first interview (OD03)

The experiences of the sample illustrate how advice from friends can often compound refugee women's lack of understanding of the legal system and lead them to seek help from unscrupulous solicitors, who do not advise them on their eligibility for legal aid funding.

Refugee women's experiences of paying for legal services were described as acerbating the stress and confusion surrounding the asylum process:

I've had one solicitor who I've paid a lot of money it was really very stressful for me (FY01)

He keep on calling, 'you owe me the money', even though I don't have money to pay him anymore (FY04)

Paying for legal support was particularly problematic for those who are destitute and have no source of income:

Experiences of legal services in Greater London

I went to this solicitor and he said he would not talk to me until I paid £600, I didn't have enough money so I paid him £20-25 at a time (KC02)

Those women who reported positive experiences of solicitors and who had been able to access legal aid funding were referred by a specialist refugee charity:

Yeah, [refugee charity] they're the one who found me a solicitor' (DN01)

They [refugee charity] got me a solicitor after some time and the solicitor was the best because she done lots of cases and she took me even though my case was not so strong (KC02)

In both of these instances, refugee charities were sensitive to the women's experiences of gender-related violence and ensured that they were seen by quality legal advisors.

Experiences of multiple solicitors

All participants had more than one solicitor assisting them with their claim for asylum, with one woman having changed solicitor five times. One woman had to find a new solicitor when her original solicitor moved jobs, whilst another's well-established relationship with her solicitor ended when the firm closed down.

In this woman's case:

I changed solicitor because my case was refused [by the Home Office]. My new solicitor has made a fresh claim and now I wait.' (KC01)

Her solicitor reportedly dropped her asylum case following the Home Office's initial refusal.

Access to solicitor services in detention

14% of women who participated in this study had been held in a detention centre in the UK as part of the asylum process. During interviews, these women were asked about their experience of accessing legal help in detention. One participant related how hard it was to find a solicitor to take on her case whilst she was in detention:

Oh my god. It's the hardest thing. They have a book in detention. You fax your details to all the firms in the UK, but most of them...maybe you'll get a handful

Experiences of legal services in Greater London

> that will reply and most of them won't take on your case. So it's very lucky they referred me to one that actually agreed to take my case and he was a good lawyer. They [the Home Office] phoned me to ask me if I had found a lawyer and I told them I haven't so they looked for one for me (OT02)

Another woman remarked that being placed in detention meant that she had to change her solicitor:

> When I was in the detention centre my solicitor was in Glasgow again.... Yeah and I have to change and he had to refer me to another solicitor to take my case while I was in detention centre (OT03)

She felt that having to change solicitor because of being placed in detention resulted in her being represented by someone 'who didn't know nothing about my case.' OT03 had only communicated with her solicitor via phone and fax:

> When I was in detention, the solicitor did not meet me at all, we were communicating by phone or by faxes (OT03)

Another woman only met with her solicitor once whilst in detention:
> We were given phones so I was able to talk to him every day, but I only got to see him once. But he would call me every day and tell me things and if there was anything I needed he would fax it whilst I was in detention (P001)

Despite only meeting with her solicitor once, P001 appeared satisfied with her communication with her solicitor when she was in detention as she was 'able to talk to him every day' and depicted him to be responsive to her needs.

Impact of dispersal on experiences of legal services

Participants were asked if they had been dispersed to other areas of the UK as part of their claim for asylum; 90% had not been moved outside of London. For the small number of refugee women who had been dispersed, being relocated to another area of the country had made access to legal services problematic:

> I was dispersed by the Home Office to Glasgow so I was living in Glasgow and the solicitor that was dealing with my case was in London and each time he need me I have to travel to London (OD03)

Experiences of legal services in Greater London

She went on to describe the difficulties she faced getting the money to pay for the journey and how the differences in law in Scotland and England eventually resulted in her needing to find a new solicitor in Glasgow:

> *When I was sent to Glasgow...we were struggling for me to come [to see my solicitor] and sometimes I don't have money to come to London for interview so they were telling me that the law in England and Glasgow is a little bit different so I have to find another lawyer over there. So in Glasgow I tried a few different firms, who didn't help me much. (OD03)*

This woman's experience illustrates the extent to which dispersal can negatively affect refugee women's access to legal services.

For those in our sample who were not dispersed, difficulty finding solicitors to take on their asylum cases because of a limited number of solicitors that process legal aid funded cases in their area meant some had to travel long distances to meet with a solicitor. One participant described the difficulties this caused in terms of travel costs and being called to see the solicitor at the last minute:

> *[We had to travel from] Portsmouth to London. In the first 6months we visited the solicitor two times. We had to pay for travel. We had to stay in London for a couple of months, the solicitor sometimes suddenly asked you to come in (WC01)*

Another woman said she had met with her solicitor in person only once:

> *She is outside in London, in Coventry. I don't see her, I saw her the first time, now she writes me emails (KC01)*

She went on to express her dissatisfaction with the communication between them:

> *We speak on the phone, we don't have enough time to speak...We communicate via email (KC01)*

This woman had been suffering with depression and appeared to be distressed and sad during the interview. Her English was very limited and she struggled to express herself. Taking these support needs into account, it is difficult to see how

Experiences of legal services in Greater London

phone and email would be an appropriate way for this woman to communicate with her solicitor.

Summary

Refugee women face multiple challenges in accessing solicitors' services in the UK. A lack of understanding of their eligibility for legal aid and relying on advice from friends often leads refugee women to pay for solicitors' services, which is particularly stressful for those who are destitute and have no source of income. Previous research has shown that refugee women are less likely to know where to seek help and advice than their male counterparts and instead to rely on 'incorrect advice from peers' (Phillimore et al., 2007:23). Specialist refugee charities play an important role in referring refugee women to legal aid solicitors who are sensitive to the needs and experiences of this vulnerable group.

The experiences of the sample suggest that it is common for refugee women to be seen by multiple solicitors during their claim for asylum, which can be problematic for a group for whom developing a trusting relationship with one professional is particularly important. Detention and dispersal can both result in refugee women having to find a new solicitor because of being moved to another region of the country. In many cases, dispersal can interrupt a refugee woman's access to solicitors' services and prevent them to developing a relationship with one solicitor. The negative impact of dispersal on access to legal services has been noted by Hobson, Cox and Sagovsky (2008), who found that this process interrupted asylum seekers' legal representation and often meant that they were unable to find new solicitors in the dispersal area.

Difficulty finding legal aid solicitors often leads to refugee women travelling long distances to meet with a solicitor and having to communicate via telephone and email rather than meeting in person, something which is challenging for those with low levels of English and who find disclosure difficult.

5.3 Communication and cultural challenges

This section explores refugee women's experiences of corresponding with solicitors once a solicitor has agreed to take on their case. The impact that poor communication with solicitors can have on this group of women, who commonly experience mental health problems as a result of the asylum process and their pre-migratory experiences will be addressed. It then provides an insight into the problems associated with children being present during interviews with solicitors.

Experiences of legal services in Greater London

Correspondence

According to the sample, poor correspondence with their solicitor was the most widely reported problem faced by refugee women when accessing legal services. Participants stated difficulties they experienced in trying to get in contact with their solicitor:

> *Not good, he [solicitor] doesn't reply to your calls, texts, emails...when maybe you'd be been given a deadline by the Home Office, so it's like you have to pester pester pester him all the time (OT02)*

> *Sometimes when I needed something I had to call so many times and he wouldn't respond and it was so frustrating (DN02)*

Another woman told us that one solicitor had not contacted her again after her case was refused by the Home Office:

> *Then when the Home Office refused me she just didn't contact me and didn't send me my papers (KC01)*

KC01 went on to describe feeling 'ignored' by this solicitor and 'frustrated' that all communication between them had ceased.

Those who had solicitors who did not communicate with them regularly about their asylum claim knew very little about the status and progress of their claims. One participant described how poor communication with her solicitor had led her to believe that an appeal had been submitted on her behalf when this was not the case:

> *He couldn't bring himself to tell me that I haven't got an appeal...So I was waiting, and I was saying I'm just waiting for the appeal, just waiting for the appeal...but I had nothing. Not until later when I got a new solicitor and they requested all of my files from the Home Office then that was when I knew, I found out in July this year that I haven't got an appeal... (DN02)*

She remarked that she now has a new solicitor who is better at explaining the process to her:

> *She [solicitor] tells me everything, when she gets a letter from the Home Office she'll call me, fax my own copy (DN02)*

Experiences of legal services in Greater London

This participant was reassured by the fact that her new solicitor kept her regularly updated on all aspects of her case and everything was explained in clear and simple terms.

Presence of children

Communication with their solicitors was impeded for some participants as a result of their children's presence during appointments. This could be distracting and prevent women from expressing themselves fully as they had to attend to their children. One participant noted that having her young daughter present during appointments with her solicitor made it difficult for her to give her solicitor her full attention:

> *I had a little child so I didn't want to take her with me because all the time she disturbs me and she doesn't give me quiet time with my solicitor and every time he would call me to come in and discuss it was a little bit difficult for me to express myself because my child was running around making noises and I have to attend her (OT03)*

This woman claimed that having her daughter present made it difficult for her to express herself because her daughter 'was running around making noises' and she was not able to have 'quiet time' with her solicitor. Childcare responsibilities have been shown to be a barrier for refugee women to access services because of a lack childcare facilities (Phillimore et al., 2007). Communication stye?

Summary

The most significant problem participants' experienced with solicitors' services was inadequate levels of correspondence with their solicitors about the status and progress of their asylum claims. This absence of communication exacerbated anxiety and depressive feelings surrounding the asylum process, and also resulted in some refugee women having very little understanding of the progress of their claim. Ineffective communication with solicitors can serve to aggravate refugee women's state of poor mental health because of the fear and uncertainty surrounding their asylum claim, which can worsen if they are not kept up to date with the progress of their claim. For this vulnerable group of women, who greatly value being listened to and being given enough time to express themselves, it is clear that there is a need for professionals to communicate more and adapt their methods of communication accordingly.

Experiences of legal services in Greater London

In some cases, communication with solicitors during appointments was also hindered by the presence of children, who can be distracting and prevent refugee women from making a full disclosure.

Notes

7   Lunar House in Croydon is the headquarters of the UK Border Agency.

Experiences of legal services in Greater London

© Nona Fara

What really matters when receiving legal and health services

6.1 Introduction

This section explores thematically refugee and asylum-seeking women's experiences of GPs and solicitors and outlines the crucial factors for effective interactions with both sets of professionals in relation to the participants' underlying mental health problems and their experiences of gender-related violence.

6.2 Building trusting relationships

During the interviews, peer researchers explored the research participants' levels of satisfaction with their interactions with GPs and solicitors. Trust was identified as a factor crucial to refugee women's relationships with solicitors and GPs. Participants reflected on the difficulties they experienced in trusting professionals as a result of their experiences in their home country. As one participant recounted:

Due to the experiences I have had before, you can't trust people it is very very hard, so you can have so many questions before you feel confident with someone, you can't really tell them your problems and maybe you don't want them to be close to you and maybe they are ok, but you are too scared (OD02)

Like other refugee women interviewed, this participant reported how hard it was for her to trust other people and related how this had an impact on her ability to open up to professionals. Other participants also expressed a reluctance to trust GPs and solicitors:

I'm not going to say yes [that I trust my solicitor], because I don't know. Because I've seen her so few times. I won't say yes for that, it's still early (DN01)

I don't trust my solicitor 100%, I've never trusted them 100%. But the way they treated me at first [welcomed me with open arms], I thought maybe they were the right people to share the experience with (DG01)

What really matters when receiving legal and health services

DN01's response, 'it's still early', reflects the time it takes for her to be able to trust professionals. For DG01, friendliness was deemed to be more significant in establishing trust in her solicitor, than their professional status. She remarked that trust was an important factor in deciding whether to 'share' her experiences with her solicitor.

Five of the refugee women reported not approaching professionals and/or services for help because of an absence of trust. One woman explained that she no longer trusted her GP to deal with her mental health problems and as a result does not go to him for help when her mental health problems become acute:

> *After that I didn't go there [to the GP] again and whenever I was feeling like that I would go to the hospital or call an ambulance (IN03)*

Another woman described how her fear and mistrust of statutory services meant that she was reluctant to seek mental health support through the NHS:

> *They [social services] said they could help me but they said they could take my daughter off me and I wasn't ready to do that so...I just had to step back from the whole thing...so thinking if I had to go to the NHS for counselling it might be really difficult you know getting my daughter, they might think I'm not a fit mum. They [NHS staff] wouldn't really understand me...I wouldn't do that, I wouldn't let them take her away from me' (DN02)*

This woman did not trust the NHS to deal with her mental health problems confidentially and so did not want to approach them for help. She feared that her involvement with NHS mental health services might negatively affect her dealings with social services: 'if I had to go to the NHS for counselling it might be really difficult you know getting my daughter, they might think I'm not a fit mum'.

Summary

Due to traumas they have experienced, refugee women can be particularly fearful of placing trust in GPs and solicitors. Participants noted that it can take a long time to build trusting relationships with these professionals. Furthermore, a lack of trust in professionals and in statutory services can result in some refugee women choosing to not engage with certain services for fear of the ramifications on their wider situation. Refugees' fear and suspicion of authorities has been widely documented (Crawley *et al.*, 2011; Kanani *et al.*, 2001; Phillimore *et al.*, 2007) and has been explained to be the result of a fear that they will be forced to return to their home country (Crawley et al., 2011).

6.3 Feeling listened to

Participants were asked whether they felt comfortable discussing personal information with GPs and solicitors and how much they felt these professionals listened to them and understood their experiences. They were also asked whether they had felt able to disclose sensitive information to their GP and solicitor and to describe the experience of doing so, as well as what might have prevented such disclosure.

Refugee women who provided positive accounts of being able to confide in professionals felt that they had been listened to:

> *When I get there I express my views, how I'm feeling and I'm listened to and that's important to me (FY02)*

> *I've had real positive experiences with my GP I met sometimes last year because they give me time and listened to my problems (LH01)*

> *It's like umm, whenever I go there I try to explain what has brought me there, he pays much attention to it and he tries to help as much as he can so that the problem is solved. I don't have any problems with that (DM01)*

However, a significant proportion of participants felt that they were not listened to by professionals:

> *There's no communication, they don't even speak to you, they don't give you a chance to speak to them (WC02)*

Feeling that she was not listened to made this woman feel frustrated. She equated not being adequately listened to with not being taken seriously:

> *I keep coming with ailments and he always thinks I'm lying (WC02)*

Another woman depicted the lack of attention she felt her GP paid her during appointments:

What really matters when receiving legal and health services

> *The GP does not look at you, they just type and look at the computer, just look at the screen and don't look at you' (KC02)*

This went on to explain that she was suffering from severe mental health problems at the time and needed specialist support. She believed her GP had not referred her to the specialist support she needed because he had not listened to her and given her his full attention.

Being given enough time

Participants spoke of the importance of being given enough time to express themselves during appointments with GPs and solicitors. Ten participants reported not having enough time with their GP during appointments and remarked that they often wished to discuss more than one health problem with their GP as well as other difficulties they experienced associated with their position as a refugee:

> *Sometimes I go to my GP and I want to explain about some other health issues and my other problems, but sometimes when you go there a GP can tell you, 'oh this is not what you're here for today you have to go and make another appointment for that'(DM01)*

> *If you go [to the GP] and he say 'what is your problem' and you tell him one, he will run for that one, he don't want another one. 'Let us see this one first', he said. 'All your problem, you cannot tell me all your problems', you have to tell one. If you have headache, I have headache, he write something for your headache and if you want to tell him you know your history and how you start your headache or something, no (CM03)*

> *I say 'oh one more thing, I've also got another problem with my back' and he says 'I can only see you for one problem at a time, you have to book another appointment to be seen about the other one' (DN02)*

The participants detailed multiple health complaints and expressed a great deal of anxiety about their health. Physical manifestations of mental distress has been described in relation to refugee women (Refugee Council, 2009), which means that this group can present a lot of physical health problems as a result of underlying mental health issues. The experiences of the above participants suggests that the time allotted for GP appointments is not adequate for refugee

What really matters when receiving legal and health services

women, who often have multiple and complex health needs and require more time to explain themselves and describe their symptoms.

Not having enough time during appointments with GPs and solicitors was especially difficult for those who had difficulty disclosing their personal story:

It took over two weeks to get the whole story across. The solicitor didn't have enough time, had other clients (WC01)

The length of time it takes to disclose personal experiences is compounded by language difficulties, which can result in refugee women needing additional time with professionals so that they are able to express themselves fully:

They should give you [refugees] extra time to express yourself because you are in a foreign country where you don't know anyone, English might not be your first language (OD02)

One participant, who spoke of how difficult it had been for her to disclose her personal history to her solicitor, reported that she had been able to cope with the experience because her solicitor had allowed her to go at her own pace:

She wanted me to take my time and everything…sometimes some things are really hard for you to talk about so if she does take her time then, when you're ready, you can keep talking about things' (DN02)

She portrayed her solicitor as wanting her to 'take her time' and explained how this was helpful 'because some things are really hard' to talk about.

Barriers to disclosure

During the interviews, participants were asked what factors had prohibited them from disclosing personal information to GPs and solicitors. One woman recalled that she had not known that she could confide in her GP about her mental health problems associated with her immigration status:

My GP, she knew…there was something disturbing me…it took so long for me to tell her about my history, what happened to me things like that, because I didn't know you could tell your GP stuff like that, I thought you had to get help somewhere else. So I was dying alone (DT01)

What really matters when receiving legal and health services

A lack of awareness of who she could go to for help meant that this woman did not know who she could disclose her experiences to. This led her to keep her situation from her GP and to suffer on her own.

Another woman stated that she had not disclosed her situation to her GP because of fear and uncertainty of how he would respond and how it would affect his treatment of her:

> *Not really because I always feel like 'cos they don't know about my case actually, cos I felt even if I had to let them know, there's this particular doctor that's always around and he doesn't know about me and he's treating me this way, so if he knows about me he might not even give me any audience or anything so I just keep quiet (DT02)*

This woman went on to tell us about the difficulties caused by not disclosing her situation to her GP:

> *Sometimes I would like to [disclose situation]* **because I do go and sign** *[reporting to the Home Office]* **every week and I do try to go but they keep asking me to bring a letter from my doctor** *[when unable to go because daughter is unwell]....but because I couldn't really discuss it with the doctor, I don't know what it's going to feel like and i don't know how they're going to treat me, I just keep quiet' (DT02)*
>
> .....
>
> *I'm kind of shy and I think if they know about me then they might be rude or not want to attend to me' (DT02)*

She detailed the Home Office as asking her to 'bring a letter' from her doctor but she was unable to request one because she did not want her GP to know that she was an asylum seeker. This account reveals the importance of refugee women making a disclosure to their GP so that they are able to provide support to a woman's wider situation, such as providing sick notes to the Home Office.

Those who told us that they had disclosed their situation as refugees to their GP and/or solicitor outlined the difficulties they had faced in doing this. One participant recalled how difficult it had been for her to recount her experiences to her solicitor:

> *Sometimes you just want to forget about your past and you don't want to remember anything and it was a bit difficult because she [solicitor] kept*

What really matters when receiving legal and health services

> *stressing it's going to help you it's going to help you so I had no choice. I had to like try and think everything back and even though I've tried not to remember most of it, it's just my past you know it can't go away it's always right in there. I tried my best (DT02)*

Her account of trying to think 'everything back' and go against her desire to 'not remember' highlights how difficult disclosure is for those who have experienced trauma. Recounting past experiences caused a great deal of stress for another woman, who told us that she had been diagnosed with PTSD and had experienced suicidal feelings:

> *I had to tell them [solicitor] the truth, I been to this country and this and this and this and I was more stressed and I was scared...so scared to go to the Home Office and sometimes I was like I don't care because my life, I didn't see that I have a life (DT01)*

Her use of repetition, 'I been to this country and this and this', implies the length of her journey to the UK and the effort involved in recounting this journey.
For some, speaking to a female professional would make disclosure easier:

> *Most of the things in my life I couldn't talk to the GP about it, I sit and waiting for one day when I can meet with a female GP so I can give more information (OD03)*

This woman stated that she would be willing to disclose 'more information' to a female GP.

Those who had been able to disclose their situation to professionals described the benefits of doing so:

> *When I told my GP, I didn't know where she would refer me on to. I just thought I will tell my GP for her to know how I am, you know. This is how I say I get help from Room to Heal, they are the one who have helped me to get the lawyers. When I came to Room to Heal, I didn't think that I would seek asylum (DN01)*

> *It is only when you give information about yourself that the doctors can help. If you don't say they won't know how to help you (LH01)*

What really matters when receiving legal and health services

For DN01, being open with her GP about her situation led her to be referred on to other services and to be helped to access other professionals. These experiences show that disclosing sensitive issues to GPs can be the first step in being referred to specialist refugee and mental health services.

Summary

Refugee women place significant value on feeling listened to and being given enough time during appointments with GPs and solicitors. Participants placed particular emphasis on appreciating those professionals who listened as opposed to those who helped solve a health problem.

As a result of their multiple health problems, a finding supported by Hickey (2011) who found that refugee women commonly suffer from mental and physical health problems, and the additional support needs associated with their immigration status, many participants said that they needed additional time during GP appointments. Participants in this study reported being told by their GPs to book another appointment to talk about other health complaints.

Refugee women also require more time with GPs and solicitors as a result of language difficulties and the time it takes for them to establish trust in professionals.

Recounting past experiences and disclosing sensitive information is extremely difficult for refugee women, especially those who have experienced trauma. This finding is supported by Bögner et al (2007) who found that those who had experienced sexual violence experienced greater difficulty in disclosing personal information during their Home Office interview. This study found that being able to disclose personal information was important for GPs and solicitors to provide participants' with the specialist medical and advocacy support they need.

A lack of awareness of who they can confide in and fear of how professionals will treat them if they disclose information about their immigration status were found to be barriers to disclosure. Trust in professionals is crucial for refugee women to disclose sensitive information about themselves.

6.4 The importance of empathy

Participants discussed what had made them feel that GPs and solicitors wanted to help them and were sympathetic with their situation as refugee women. Those who reported feeling they had been listened to and understood, told of instances when professionals had displayed emotional understanding for their situation:

What really matters when receiving legal and health services

I think so, she understood me very well due to her response, like whenever I was trying to tell her, it's like 'oh sorry'...that made me feel that she was very very understanding of what I was talking about' (DG01)

He understood it very well, he was understanding, compassionate (OD02)

[She was] emotional, cried. You can see her eyes, she's wiping them... she was like showing me emotional understanding, you know. She also tearing, you know like crying...I won't complain about her (DN01)

Participants placed a particular emphasis on the immediate verbal or physical response a professional gave when they disclosed their situation, indicating the significance of displays of empathy.

No display of empathy from her GP made one participant feel that her mental health needs had not been taken seriously:

I was having psychological problems which I received treatment for, for years. I was feeling really disturbed and ill and I was trembling. And when I went there in that state he acted like he saw the devil or something! And once he actually told me that I was pretending and abusing the situation (IN03)

This woman felt that her GP had not empathised with her mental health condition. Her phrase 'acted like he saw the devil' implies that his response to her condition made her feel that he neither believed nor understood her condition.

Assumptions around ethnicity

The issue of a professionals' ethnicity was highlighted by six of the refugee women interviewed. In particular, they expressed a preference for GPs and solicitors from an ethnic minority background because they perceive them as being more likely to empathise with their experiences. Those who expressed a preference for ethnic minority professionals believed that they have a better awareness of their experiences in their home country and as an immigrant in the UK:

Like my GP that I am seeing now she is not English she is Asian, so I think she understands when people struggle than some people don't, some doctors don't. They might have gone through it themselves in the past so they can relate to what women go through easily (LH01)

What really matters when receiving legal and health services

I think even my GP she's lived in one of these countries outside, so I think she knows about all these things, she was like showing me emotional understanding, you know (DN01)

*[My solicitor was] **very understanding - she was ethnic minority background** (WC01)*

Participants' assumptions about professionals, their ethnicity and their life experiences led them to assume that those from an ethnic minority background are more likely to understand what life is like in their country of origin and empathise with the experiences they have had.

Some women reported positive experiences with professionals from the same country of origin:

*Yeah, I think he did [understand my experiences] **because he's from Uganda as well so he's heard about these things, he already knew about these things that I was telling him.** He had some information about what I was trying to tell him (PM01)*

***She knew exactly what was going on in my country** so yeah, it's like, whenever I try to explain to her it wasn't new in her ears, she knew (DG01)*

What seems crucial from both of these accounts is the knowledge that both PM01 and DG01's solicitors had about the participants' home countries and how this enabled them to emphasise with the women's personal experiences.

Awareness of wider support needs

Research participants commented that professionals who were aware of and sensitive to their wider support needs, such as their asylum claim and mental health problems, were able to act as vital advocates for them when liaising with other professionals as well as helping them to access additional support by referring them to specialist services:

*She [GP] was really keen on my health and **she even used to write letters to the Home Office about my mental health and all this…..She referred me to Refugee Therapy** (KC02)*

What really matters when receiving legal and health services

Another woman felt that her solicitor was sensitive to her needs because she referred her to further support and made sure that she was supported and felt in control throughout this process:

I would say I do trust her cos she's been really good and very helpful and she makes me understand things. Even if she has to refer me to another organisation or some other people she'll let me know and make me feel comfortable and says that if I don't feel comfortable with them I should let her know and sometimes if I don't want to go to their office she normally arrange for them to come down to her or the office where I feel more comfortable where we can talk about things (DT02)

This woman's solicitor is reported as giving her a great deal of choice and flexibility with her contact with other organisations, demonstrating an understanding of the difficulties she might face with trusting and opening up to people she does not know. Her description of being able to give feedback and have control over her experiences of the service was crucial to her positive experience.

One participant recounted when her solicitor had not been sensitive to her situation as an asylum seeker and did not advocate on her behalf:

In Finchley there's a drop in and they want letters from our solicitors to say that our cases are still pending umm I call this man [solicitor] I don't know how many times, just to email those people ...he never (FY04)

She expressed frustration that her solicitor did not get in touch with a drop-in centre despite her efforts to prompt him. In this instance, the solicitor's inaction suggests a lack of care and sensitivity to their client's additional support needs.

A large proportion of the women interviewed highlighted the importance of professionals having an awareness of their mental health needs:

Because some solicitors when women go there, like me who has bad experiences in my country, yeah, like I needed someone, I needed therapists, I needed counsellors, I really needed some other people to talk to other than the solicitors...some solicitors don't take it as a serious issue, then at the end of the day when things go bad they realise 'oh this person really needed it' (DG01)

What really matters when receiving legal and health services

> [GPs should know] *that we need counselling, we need to be listened to and helped as refugees who are mentally affected. The ones I've seen do not care about your background, they're not sensitive enough and they treat you as a normal person who hasn't experienced hardships (WC02)*

> *They need to understand more about our mental health needs (IN02)*

For WC02, it was important for her GP to have a good understanding of her mental health needs so that she could be provided with the appropriate support.

Another participant described the importance of GPs having a sound understanding of her experiences:

> *Sometimes I was going through tough things; I was depressed and didn't have anyone to talk to. And being a doctor they should understand where you're coming from (DN02)*

She told of how her mental health problems, coupled with her social isolation, meant that she wished for her GP to have a greater understanding of her position.

The significance of gender

Whilst for some, the gender of their GP and solicitor did not affect their experiences, eighteen of the refugee women interviewed expressed a preference to be seen by a professional of the same gender:

> *Because you know, she is a woman, woman for woman. She had a big heart, you know. She really felt, just like a woman (CD01)*

> *Yes, very [understanding] because she is a female so she understands more my problems and she is a very compassionate solicitor, I wish I had one like that before (OD03)*

CD01's expression 'woman for woman' suggests a mirroring of experiences and understanding between those of the same gender. Furthermore, her use of the words 'she had a big heart' and 'just like a woman' suggests a perception that women are more able to relate to her experiences.

There was an assumption amongst a significant proportion of the sample that the commonality of experience between them and female professionals resulted in an increased level of understanding between them; something that was not seen to be as easy to achieve with men. When asked whether she had felt able to speak to her male GP about personal, sensitive issues, one woman replied:

No, because he's a man, we've no connection (WC02)

This woman's use of the word 'connection' suggests that she felt there was an inherent lack of understanding between her and her GP as a result of a difference in gender. Where there was a preference to be seen by a professional of the same gender, participants reported a lack of confidence in men's ability to understand their experiences and also that neither side would feel comfortable openly discussing certain topics:

I want my solicitor to be a woman because I'm a woman. Having a man, I would not explain myself in some details because, for example, I had a problem with my husband back in Africa, I cannot explain to him because he will not understand so I think that the problem I had with the first solicitor, because he was a man and he did not really understand, he didn't ask me the right questions so he can't get how to help me, he was not free with me so he cannot really ask the important questions (KC02)

This woman's perception of the competence of her solicitor is inherently linked with his gender. She expressed frustration that her first solicitor, a man, had not asked her pertinent questions related to her claim for asylum and she saw this as a result of his lack of understanding of her situation as a woman and his inability to speak candidly and openly about sensitive topics.

For sensitivity reasons, participants were not directly asked whether they had experienced gender-related violence. Many women also chose not to disclose the reasons why they had left their home country and sought asylum in the UK. Of those who were willing to discuss this with us, two women from Uganda said they had experienced persecution because of their sexuality, two disclosed that they had been raped, one woman told us that she fled an abusive domestic situation and one woman was currently experiencing domestic violence in a relationship in the UK. One woman who had experienced gender-related violence explained the impact this had had on her relationship with professionals:

What really matters when receiving legal and health services

> *Because of my background, I would like to meet with a female GP, who will understand maybe my problem, because it's a gynaecological problem as well. I was raped so I've got a lot of things to say, I won't feel comfortable in front of a male GP to talk about it* (OD03)

For this woman, her experience of rape made it difficult for her to confide in a male GP. She told us that she is still waiting to be seen by a female GP to disclose her experiences. As well as saying that she would not be 'comfortable' discussing her experiences with a man, she also perceived that a GP's ability to understand her 'gynaecological' problems was inherently linked with their gender. Another woman spoke about her fear of being seen by male GPs and solicitors as a result of her experience of gender-related violence:

> *In my case and what happened to me, I didn't want to see any men in my life. I don't want to see men . I don't want anything to do with men...that's why when you come here [refugee charity] you get the counselling you get it with just women. So I'm trying slowly slowly to be strong'* (DN01)
>
> ...
>
> *My psychiatrist, he's a man; I was scared of him the first time I had to go in the room with him. He noticed something the first time. The second time I went in with a trainee psychiatrist, a woman. Today I had an appointment with him, I thought there was going to be someone else in the room. But I was told by someone else that he's very good and he's the top psychiatrist so I shouldn't be scared of him. But I was scared. You know it's like you're going to tell someone your story and he's a man, and there are men who messed up your life, you know what I mean so, you they are looking at you and they see what was there, I don't know, that's my mind'* (DN02)

This woman related how difficult it is for her to disclose her experience to a man and to be alone in a room with male professionals because of the gender-specific nature of her experiences. She described herself as feeling vulnerable in the presence of men and as having developed a deep distrust and fear of the opposite sex and therefore preferred an all-female environment. Communication style?

Summary

Displays of empathy from GPs and solicitors were reported to be vital for refugee women as a result of the traumas they have experienced, the prevalence of mental

What really matters when receiving legal and health services

health problems amongst this group and the isolation they experience in the UK. It was found that demonstrations of empathy helped with disclosure as it made participants feel more accepted and understood.

Refugee women feel more empathised with when GPs and solicitors communicate an awareness of the situation in their country of origin. There is a preference amongst some refugee women to be seen by GPs and solicitors from an ethnic minority background or from their own country of origin as this augments the degree to which they feel empathised with. It is beneficial for professionals to have a sound awareness of refugee women's wider situation and needs in order that they can be sensitive to their additional support needs and have an understanding of the advocacy role they must often play on behalf of refugee women.

Some refugee women prefer to be seen by female GPs and solicitors because of a perception that they are better able to empathise with their experiences as women. The effectiveness of same-gender interviewing officers and professionals on asylum-seekers' willingness to disclose experiences of sexual violence has been revealed by Bögner et al. (2009). A lack of commonality of experience with men means that some refugee women feel that male professionals are unable to empathise with their experiences relating to their gender and this is perceived to act as a barrier to open and frank communication with professionals of a different gender. The gender of GPs and solicitors is particularly significant for those who have experienced gender-related violence, who can feel uncomfortable discussing their experiences with men. Previous research found that refugee women, who have experienced sexual violence are often 'reluctant to speak to white male GPs about their experiences' (Phillimore et al., 2007:26). For some participants in this study, their experiences of gender-related violence resulted in an entrenched mistrust and fear of men, making it traumatic for them to be seen by and to disclose personal information to male professionals.

A commonality of experience, both as a result of a shared gender or ethnicity, increases the level of trust refugee women have for GP and solicitors and this in turn aids with disclosure. Communication stye?

 What really matters when receiving legal and health services

© IARS

Discussion and recommendations

7.1 Introduction

This study provides insight into refugee women's experiences of GP[8] and solicitor services in Greater London in light of the prevalence of experiences of gender-related violence amongst this group (Dorling et al., 2012) and the added physical and mental health problems they face as a result (Refugee Council, 2009).

The user-led approach of this study created a sensitive and supportive environment and better enabled participants to frankly communicate their experiences. The openness of the participants provides a rich and in-depth vision of what refugee women require from GPs and solicitors and what enables them to access the services and support they need.

From the evidence presented, it is possible to begin to formulate the crucial elements of a gender-sensitive approach to working with this group of women. The research locates the perspectives of refugee women within the current policy context of ensuring that refugee women who are victims of gender-related violence receive appropriate support and raising awareness amongst practitioners of the prevalence of gender-related violence in refugee communities.

The findings from the fieldwork are a stark reminder of the vulnerability of this group of women in Britain. The United Nations have stated that 'refugee women are affected [by sexual and gender based violence] more than any other women's population in the world' (United Nations, 2008). When working with this group it is incumbent upon service providers to keep in mind that refugee women in the UK come from countries 'with high levels of sexual violence' and from countries where 'sexual violence by security forces has been institutionalised' (Refugee Council, 2009:4).

Inherent in refugee women's' positive experiences of GP and solicitor services as outlined in this study are the human rights-based principles of fairness, respect, equality, dignity and autonomy. Gavrielides (2008:201) examined the role of human rights principles in 'determining and improving customer satisfaction with public services'. This study confirms the instrumental role of these principles as 'drivers' to improve experiences of service provision, particularly amongst vulnerable

Discussion and recommendations

groups, such as refugee women. The recommendations of this study should be seen in relation to the obligation of public authorities to act in accordance with the 1950 European Convention on Human Rights and for public officials to take human rights into account in their day-to-day work (Ministry of Justice, 2006).

In order for refugee women to receive services that are sensitive to their personal needs, service providers need to adopt a positive approach to ensuring equality outcome for this group rather than simply equality of opportunity to access service; the following recommendations detail what such an approach entails.

7.2 The importance of building trust and communicating empathy

A key finding from the fieldwork was the difficulty refugee women experience in developing trusting relationships with GPs and solicitors. Trust was identified as crucial to a refugee woman's ability to disclose sensitive information. For this group of women, who have often suffered a great deal of trauma, it can take a long time to develop trust in others, particularly those in authority. According to five participants, where there was a lack of trust in professionals and a lack of confidence that the service would help them, this resulted in their withdrawal from services and choosing to look after themselves rather than approaching professionals for help. It is important for GPs and solicitors to establish trust with the refugee women they work with in order to encourage disclosure of sensitive information, which may be crucial to receiving specialist support. Those professionals who do not develop trusting relationships with refugee women are at risk of neglecting those who need help because they do not feel able to disclose vital information. There is an opportunity to identify those in need of specialist support early on by creating an environment suitable for such a disclosure.

Refugee women who had been able to discuss personal information with their GP and/or solicitor, including pre-migratory experiences and the nature of their current situation in the UK, outlined the positive impact of feeling listened to and of professionals outwardly communicating empathy for their situation. Being able to disclose sensitive personal information to GPs and solicitors enables these professionals to provide them with specialist medical and advocacy support that they need. Refugee women reported feeling more empathised with when professionals demonstrated an awareness of the situation in their country of origin. An understanding of the situation of refugees living in the UK is also

Discussion and recommendations

beneficial for professionals to have an understanding of refugee women's additional support needs and the advocacy role they often need to play on behalf of this group. Without professionals who make them feel listened to and empathised with, it is unlikely that refugee women will openly communicate their experiences. In addition, a lack of understanding of the experiences of refugee women both in their countries of origin and in the UK means that professionals are unable to provide support, which takes a woman's wider welfare needs into account.

Participants placed particular emphasis on appreciating those GPs who listened as opposed to those who helped solve a health problem. This finding suggests that refugee women are in need of more therapeutic support from mental health services. Counselling has been found to be an unmet need for refugees who are victims of torture and rape (Refugee Council, 2005) and the lack of early psychotherapeutic interventions in initial accommodation have been criticised (Querton, 2012).

Whilst a need for increased referrals to mental health services has been noted, this study shows the need for changes to the way that GPs interact with refugee women patients due to their difficulties with trust. Rather than providing equality of *opportunity* to benefit from a standard service, if GPs want to ensure equality of *outcome* for refugee women patients then they need to utilise counselling techniques, such as active listening and communicating empathy, to develop the trust necessary for these patients to disclose important information.

Recommendation: Health Education England and the newly formed Local Education and Training Boards along with authorised CPD providers accredited through the Solicitors Regulation Authority should ensure that current and future GPs and solicitors receive training on working sensitively with refugee women; who have experienced gender-related violence. This training should develop professionals' understanding of the mental and physical health needs of this group and provide an awareness of refugee women's pre and post-migration experiences. Training of this nature would enable professionals to work considerately with refugee women and to identify those women, who require specialist support.

7.3 A need for more time

The need for refugee women to be provided with more time during appointments with GPs and solicitors emerged as a further finding from this study. As a result of their difficulties recounting past experiences and

Discussion and recommendations

disclosing sensitive information and their low levels of English, this group of women require more time when first establishing a relationship with professionals. Experiences of the sample highlight the significance of encouraging full disclosure as it can mean that professionals are able to provide them with specialist support.

The need for longer appointments with GPs when a refugee woman first registers is particularly acute as a result of refugee women's often multiple and complex health needs. If more time were provided with GPs at the beginning of the relationship, this would allow refugee women to detail their health concerns and explain their experiences at a pace they feel comfortable with, feel listened to, encourage the disclosure of particularly sensitive information and lay the foundations of a trusting relationship.

The Refugee Council's 2013 report 'When Maternity Doesn't Matter', which explores the impact of dispersal on pregnant asylum-seeking women, also highlights the importance of refugee women having enough time during appointments with healthcare professionals. Midwives interviewed for the study reported that 'it took time to build relationships that would make the women secure enough to disclose personal details...especially if they had experienced trauma or abuse or had other mental health problems' (Feldman, 2013:45). The Council on Social Action (2009:16) support the view that a lack of time during appointments with solicitors can be detrimental for asylum-seekers' claims for asylum: 'the failure to give the full story at initial stage due to solicitor's time constraints...leads to greater problems at interview and appeal stages where these details are required, and prolongation of the case'. Although there are multiple barriers to refugee women disclosing sensitive personal information, allowing more time during appointments for this group would go some way to facilitate disclosure.

Refugee women face multiple barriers to expressing themselves and divulging sensitive personal information. Therefore, to expect this group to be able to benefit from these services to the same extent as the average service user is unrealistic unless they are given more time during appointments with GPs and solicitors. It might be argued that providing this group with more time is too costly for both areas of service provision. However, achieving the best outcome for refugee women may be more costly in the long run if they are not provided with enough time during their initial appointments with GPs and solicitors. For instance, refugee women may frequently book GP appointments because an underlying mental health need has not been addressed and a solicitor may need to start afresh with a client's asylum claim if there is a late disclosure of important information.

Discussion and recommendations

Recommendation: The Legal Services Board should review the current funding and payments systems for publicly funded immigration and asylum work to enable solicitors to spend more time with clients at the beginning of their claim.

Recommendation: GP practices should provide double appointments for a refugee woman's first appointment with the GP and thereafter promote the option of booking double appointments to refugee women patients who require more time.

Recommendation: NHS Commissioning Boards in areas of high refugee populations should consider the establishment of specialist services to meet the needs of refugee communities and are able to provide more time per patient.

7.4 The importance of the gender

The appropriate use of same-gender professionals in both GP and solicitors services is crucial to a gender-sensitive approach to working with refugee women. Whilst for some, the gender of their GP and solicitor did not affect their experiences, twelve of the refugee women who participated in this study expressed a preference for a female GP and six stated a preference for a female solicitor. There was an assumption amongst a significant proportion of the sample that the commonality of experience between themselves and female professionals resulted in an increased level of understanding between them; something that was not deemed to be as easy to achieve with men.

The gender of GPs and solicitors is particularly significant for those who had experienced gender-related violence as they often felt uncomfortable discussing their experiences with men. For some, their experiences of gender-related violence resulted in an entrenched mistrust and fear of men, making it traumatic for them to be seen by and to disclose personal information to male professionals. One woman explained that her experience of being raped made it difficult for her to confide in a male GP and another woman expressed frustration at being seen by a male solicitor with whom she was not able to speak candidly and openly about sensitive topics. Research conducted by Bögner *et al.* (2009) supports this view, finding that same-gender interviewing officers and interviewers in asylum interviews to have a positive effect upon an asylum-seekers' willingness to disclose experiences of sexual violence.

The barriers that refugee women face to disclosing sensitive personal information mean that the absence of a disclosure should not be taken as evidence of not having suffered from gender-related violence. It is therefore essential that

Discussion and recommendations

refugee women are consistently provided with the choice of being seen by a female professional, not just during asylum interviews, but when accessing GP and solicitor services in order to encourage disclosure. For those who have experienced gender-related violence it is particularly important to reduce the risk of re-traumatisation.

Recommendation: As a matter of procedure, GP and solicitor's services should give refugee women a choice regarding the gender of the professionals that they come into contact with so as to ensure that those women, who may not have already disclosed their experiences of gender-related violence, have the option of an all-female environment.

7.5 Problems with registering with GP practices

The need for all refugee women to have consistent access to GP services emerged as a significant finding from this research. The experiences of the sample indicate that *asylum-seeking* women in particular commonly experience problems with registering with GP services as a result of some practices refusing to register new patients who are unable to provide proof-of-address documentation, as well as a lack of understanding on behalf of some reception staff of asylum-seekers' entitlements to primary health care. As noted by the British Medical Association (2012:3): 'it can often be difficult for asylum-seekers and refused asylum seekers to produce certain types of documentation such as passports or utility bills'. The Royal College for General Practitioners' recent position statement also noted that 'there is still considerable misunderstanding at a local level [in regards to] who is eligible to register with a General Practitioner' (Royal College of General Practitioners, 2013).

Inconsistencies in refugee women's experiences of registering with GP practices reflect the differences in practice between different GP practices regarding the registration of asylum-seeking patients. One asylum-seeking woman told us that she had not been registered with a GP for three years because she was not able to find a GP practice that would register her. Ready access to primary health care is of vital importance to this group of women, whose mental and physical health needs are often multiple and complex. Removing barriers for refugee women from gaining full registration with a GP practice would decrease delays in refugee women's access to healthcare and ensure that they are provided with the healthcare to which they are entitled.

Discussion and recommendations

Difficulties with registering with GP practices are compounded for those who move house frequently or do not have a permanent address. According to the experiences of the sample, some refugee women choose to remain with an old GP practice despite moving areas because of the difficulties associated with finding a GP practice that will register them. This results in some women travelling long distances for appointments. Creating a culture of inclusion where all GP practices are known to accept asylum-seekers and refused asylum-seekers as patients would enable refugee women to register with a different GP when they move to a new area.

The decision of some GP practices to prevent the registration of new patients, who are unable to provide proof-of-address documentation, can result in the exclusion of asylum seekers from primary healthcare. This exclusion is at odds with the founding principles of the NHS, which state that healthcare should meet the needs of everyone. Indeed, The NHS Constitution (2011:6) states that all have the right 'not to be discriminated against in the provision of NHS services including on the grounds of gender, race, disability, age, sexual orientation, religion, belief...'. A British Medical Association (2004) survey with GPs detailed the challenges of having asylum-seeking patients on their patient lists. These disincentives must be addressed at a commissioning level so that it is not the asylum seekers themselves who suffer. Whilst some GP practices continue to exclude asylum-seekers from their patient registers, entitlement to primary healthcare continues to be a postcode lottery for this group. A more humane approach to registering new patients is needed as well as incentives for practices to register asylum-seeking patients.

Recommendation: Clear guidance should be issued to reception staff and GP practice managers regarding refugee and asylum-seekers' entitlements to healthcare and what types of documentation can be reasonably asked for as proof of address. We support the BMA's view that 'practices should therefore use their discretion and consider the individual circumstances of prospective patients when asking for identification' (British Medical Association, 2012:3).

7.6 Consistency of healthcare

The importance of being able to establish a trusting relationship with *one* GP arose as a substantial finding from this study. Many participants often had to see several different doctors at the same GP practice and this made it

Discussion and recommendations

challenging for them to build a relationship where disclosure of sensitive information was possible. For refugee women, the difficulties associated with being seen by different GPs included having to re-tell their stories to different doctors and being repeatedly asked questions that reminded them of their past. It is vital that once a refugee woman has confided in a GP or has been asked questions that remind her of traumatic experiences that she not put in a situation where she will be asked to repeat this information when not strictly necessary. The development of relationships where GPs have a good understanding of refugee women's individual experiences is crucial for effective communication between patient and doctor and for GPs to be able to make decisions about a refugee woman's care, which are informed by an appreciation for her wider circumstances. For this reason, GP practices that do not ensure that female refugee patients are assigned to one GP and do not take care that they are seen by their registered GP as much as possible, are in danger of putting some of their most vulnerable patients at risk of developing further health problems and well as having existing conditions go untreated. When it is necessary for refugee women patients to be seen by different GPs, sensitivity should be taken to share knowledge between doctors within the same practice so that refugee women patients are not required to re-tell their story each time they see a different GP.

For those who move house frequently or do not have a permanent place to stay, it can be difficult to build a relationship with the same GP as they are required to register with a new GP practice whenever they move area. One woman explained that she found it really hard to adjust when she had to register with a new GP when she moved house. This group of vulnerable women can often lead transient lifestyles as a result of homelessness, destitution and frequently being moved by Home Office. This transience can negatively impact a refugee woman's experience of healthcare as it interrupts established relationships with GPs, who, with a good understanding of their past experiences and current situation, can provide them with specialist support.

Recommendation: Care must be taken at an local practice level to ensure that refugee women receive continuity of care and are seen by the same GP as much as is possible. GP practices must provide clear information upon registration about whether they match patients with one GP and about the days each doctor works/what clinics they run so that patients know how to ensure they see the same GP. When deciding which GP with whom to register a female refugee patient, consideration should be taken to the GP's contracted hours/days of work.

Discussion and recommendations

Recommendation: GP practices should create mechanisms to ensure that all GPs within the same practice are aware of vulnerable patients, such as refugee women, and to make sure that these patients are not placed in situations where they will be asked insensitive questions, which they may find difficult to discuss.

Recommendation: GP practices should issue hand held health records for refugee women patients in order to protect against the interruptions to healthcare that take place as a result of this group's transient lifestyle and ensure some continuity of care. Clear information must be given to refugee women patients about the availability of hand held medical records and the importance of taking them when registering with a new GP.

7.7 Provision of language support services in GP services

A further key finding from this study was that low levels of English language existed even amongst those research participants who had lived in the UK for 10 years or more. This finding is supported by research conducted by Gammell *et al.* (1993), which found that women refugees are less likely to speak English than their male counterparts. The difficulties some refugee women experienced in communicating with GPs resulted in them not being able to fully express themselves or comprehend the nature of the medication they had been prescribed. One woman told us that her difficulties with English affected her ability to communicate with her GP and meant that she was not able to tell her GP 'the whole story'. The difficulties experienced by some of the sample are indicative of discrepancies in GPs' use of language support services. This finding is corroborated by research published by Mind (2009:18), which reports that inconsistencies exist in regards to the provision of interpreting services within GP practices and that 'many GP practices still do not provide interpreting services for patients'. Without language support refugee women are unable to fully express themselves and there is also a danger of misdiagnosis as a result of miscommunication.

Those refugee women who had experienced using interpreting services for appointments with their GP reported mixed experiences. Whilst some of the women who participated in this study reported positive experiences of using interpreters, some expressed dissatisfaction over the quality of the interpreting and concern that their meaning had not been properly communicated to the GP. The experiences of the sample suggest that refugee women experience difficulties in trusting

Discussion and recommendations

interpreters to communicate their needs accurately. Assurance regarding the quality of interpreting is of utmost importance for this vulnerable group, due to the difficulties they face in disclosing sensitive information and re-telling their personal stories. Furthermore, given the difficulties this group face in trusting those in authority, it is not surprising that they face problems trusting interpreters to discuss sensitive information on their behalf. Therefore, it is vital that GPs play a role in facilitating a trusting relationship between patient and interpreter.

Recommendation: Staff in GP practices should be issued clear guidance around accessing interpreting services and must ensure that professional interpreters are provided for all patients who need them.

Recommendation: Training should be provided to GPs on how to use interpreters when working with refugee women with particular emphasis on refugee women who have experienced gender-related violence. This training should include how to explain the interpreting process to patients and offer patients the opportunity to give feedback about their experiences of interpreters to ensure patient satisfaction.

7.8 The use of informal interpreters in GP services

Problems associated with the use of informal interpreters, such as family members, were identified through this study. However, this proved difficult for those refugee women with no family or support network in the UK. Using children to interpret was also sometimes conveyed as problematic as it can hinder open communication with GPs on sensitive topics. Downing and Roat (2002) describe the disadvantages to this interpreting approach as including: a lack of language skills on behalf of the informal interpreter; a lack of confidentiality and damage to family relationships, particularly children. A refugee woman who participated in this study recalled feeling embarrassed when she used her daughter as an interpreter because she did not feel comfortable saying 'everything in front of my children'. Care must be taken that *professional* interpreters are used at all times to protect against the use of informal interpreters, whose presence may negatively impact on a refugee woman's ability to express herself. Although some participants in this study reported that they did not mind using family members to interpret, GPs should make sure that professional interpreting services are always used to protect against any undisclosed experiences of gender-related violence.

Discussion and recommendations

The ease of using informal interpreters and some women's willingness to use family members to interpret on their behalf should obscure the danger of this form of interpreting. The diversity of experience –all are different.

Recommendation: The use of informal interpreters in GP practices must cease and GPs should not encourage the use of family and/friends as informal interpreters as a 'quick-fix' approach to meeting language support needs.

Recommendation: NHS commissioners in areas of high refugee populations should consider using a modified Quality and Outcomes Framework (QOF) to incentivise GP practices to provide professional interpreting services to those who need them.

7.9 Awareness of entitlement to legal aid

According to the experiences of our sample, a lack of understanding of their rights and entitlements to legal aid as well as poor advice from friends leads refugee women to seek help from solicitors, who charge them for their services. 20% of the women interviewed said that they had paid for a solicitor because they had not been made aware of their eligibility for legal aid and the majority were referred by friends. Most of these women had paid a solicitor for their initial claim for asylum and had then gone on to access a legal aid solicitor to submit an appeal or a fresh claim, indicating that there is a lack of information on their entitlements at the start of the asylum process. Paying for legal support is particularly problematic for those who are destitute and have no source of income; one woman told us that she had to pay her solicitor in instalments of £20-25 at a time. The stress and confusion surrounding the asylum process is exacerbated by the anxiety of having to pay for a solicitor and some women described being harassed by solicitors asking them for money. This study found that refugee women seem to be getting conflicting and potentially incorrect information about funding their claims for asylum. There's a danger that the complexity of the asylum process is being exploited by unscrupulous solicitors, who benefit from asylum-seeking women's lack of awareness of their rights.

It is of upmost importance that refugee women are provided with clear information on their eligibility for legal aid at the beginning of the asylum process. Currently the Home Office provides this information in a port of claim leaflet entitled, 'Important Information about your Asylum Claim', which includes a section on legal advice. However, research conducted by Asylum Aid found that

Discussion and recommendations

'there were very few asylum seekers who had this leaflet with them when they arrived in initial accommodation', thus indicating that there is inconsistent and inadequate provision of information to asylum-seekers regarding legal aid at the Asylum Screening Unit (Querton, 2012:55).

Recommendation: The Home Office should ensure that all asylum-seekers are *consistently* provided with clear information and advice on their rights and entitlements to legal aid and how to find a legal aid solicitor at the Asylum Screening Unit. The current port of claim leaflet should be amended to include clearer guidance regarding asylum seekers' eligibility for legal aid.

7.10 The impact of detention and dispersal on access on solicitors' services

The difficulties refugee women face in accessing legal aid solicitors are compounded by detention and dispersal; both can result in refugee women having to find a new solicitor because they have been moved to another area of the country. Although the majority of the women we interviewed had not been dispersed outside of London, the small number of women who had been dispersed reported that it had made access to legal services problematic. Dispersal can result in refugee women travelling long distances to meet with a solicitor, which they are required to pay for.

Dispersal can interrupt refugee women's access to solicitors' services and contribute to the prevalence of refugee women being seen by multiple solicitors, which can be problematic for a group for whom developing a trusting relationship with one professional is particularly important. It is vital that once refugee women have established a relationship with one solicitor that this relationship is not interrupted as a result of dispersal or being placed in detention.

Both dispersal and detention are common experiences for those seeking asylum in this country. These aspects of the asylum process should not obstruct a refugee woman's access to solicitor services, which aids her in her search for liberty and establishment of a new life. Those who are dispersed and/or detained should not be put at a disadvantage in their claim for asylum because it has interrupted their access to solicitor services.

Recommendation: Asylum-seeking women should not be dispersed to locations far away from their solicitors if a relationship has already been established. Where

Discussion and recommendations

this is unavoidable, the Home Office should provide additional cash support for asylum-seeking women to attend legal appointments.

7.11 A shortage of legal aid solicitors

This study found that a shortage of legal aid solicitors who will take on asylum cases means that refugee women often have to travel long distances to meet with a solicitor. In some cases this meant that participants had to communicate with their solicitor via telephone and email; something which is challenging for those with low levels of English and who find disclosure difficult. The shortage of solicitors practicing immigration law has been widely noted (Muggeridge & Maman, 2011; Hobson, Cox, & Sagovsky, 2008b). Muggeridge & Maman (2011) have highlighted not only a lack of solicitors willing to take on asylum cases, but also a regional disparity in the availability of solicitors: 'a regional pattern emerged that access to legal representation is not uniform across the UK', with many refugee women having to travel out of their region and into London to meet with a solicitor (ibid: 42). It is important that refugee women, who experience difficulties in developing trusting relationships with professionals and in disclosing sensitive personal information, are able to meet with their solicitor in person at a location close to their accommodation. It is unacceptable for refugee women to communicate with their solicitor via telephone and/or email, especially for those with low levels of English language ability.

Shortages of solicitors practicing immigration law are set to worsen with the impact of the 2012 Legal Aid, Sentencing and Punishment of Offenders Act, which came into force in April 2013. Although asylum cases remain in scope for legal aid funding, there is concern about the impact of this piece of legislation on asylum-seekers' access to legal aid as a result of the impact of the bill on those who provide legal advice, who will lose funding as a result of these changes (Refugee Council, 2011b). In addition, the government has recently announced proposals to cut £220m more from the £1.7bn legal aid budget (Ministry of Justice, 2013). In order for the asylum process to remain fair and non-discriminatory it is vital that asylum seeking women, who are commonly destitute, have access to quality free legal advice. Without quality legal advice, refugee women, many of whom are victims of gender-related persecution, will not receive the specialist help they urgently need. Asylum Aid (2011:3) argue that recent cuts to legal aid are not 'gender-neutral' as refugee women often have more 'complex immigration and protection needs' and as more 'economically disadvantaged' are 'less likely to be

Discussion and recommendations

able to pay a solicitor for legal advice'. The author supports Asylum Aid's (2011) view that more cross-sector working within government is required to ensure that high quality legal advice is available to asylum-seeking women across the UK.

Recommendation: There should be increased cross-sector working between the Home Office and the Legal Services Board to ensure that refugee women are not dispersed to areas of the UK where there is limited access to legal aid immigration solicitors. Dispersal areas should be chosen in light of the provision of specialist legal aid advice services.

7.12 A need for better correspondence with solicitors

A further key finding was the problems refugee women reported in relation to corresponding with their solicitor about their asylum case. The women interviewed reported inadequate levels of correspondence on the behalf of their solicitors in regards to the status and progress of their asylum claims. One woman spoke of feeling frustrated because she had to continually pester her solicitor to respond to her. Another woman told us that one solicitor had stopped all communication with her after her claim had been refused. This absence of communication aggravates anxiety and depressive feelings surrounding the asylum process and can also result in refugee women having very little understanding about the progress of their claim. The experiences of the sample indicate that some solicitors to do not take the vulnerability of asylum-seeking women into consideration when dealing with their cases. Refugee women must be provided with clear information about their asylum claim on a regular basis. Solicitors must respond to their refugee women clients promptly and keep them up-to-date with the progress of their case. Research conducted by Trude & Gibbs (2010) support the view that regular communication with asylum-seeking clients is of utmost importance: 'Access to the representative is an essential part of the process for clients. Representatives should be directly available to respond to clients within a reasonable time frame' (ibid:8). Their study found that 'Clients appreciated a range of means of contact such as telephone, email and written correspondence as appropriate' (ibid).

Recommendation: The Solicitor's Regulation Authority should ensure that there is training provision for solicitors working with asylum seekers on good practice in corresponding with asylum-seeking clients with special consideration for the

Discussion and recommendations

needs of refugee women. This good practice would include demonstrating an awareness of the needs and expectations of this vulnerable group and managing these expectations in a considerate and transparent manner.

7.13 The presence of children in solicitor appointments

Our study also found that communication between refugee women and solicitors during appointments can be hindered by the presence of children, who were depicted as a distracting presence and as preventing refugee women from speaking confidentially with their solicitor. Refugee women must be provided with privacy when meeting with their solicitor in order to be able to discuss sensitive information. Those women who are not able to speak privately with their solicitor without their children present are at risk of not disclosing information that may be pertinent to their claim for asylum. It is vital that refugee women with children are not put at a disadvantage in their claim for asylum because they have not been able to speak privately with their solicitor. Providing these women with the means to access free childcare services would provide them with the choice of whether to bring their children to solicitor appointments.

Recommendation: The Home Office should revise the level of financial support provided to asylum-seeking women with young children below school age, who are assessed to be destitute, to include the provision of childcare vouchers so that they are not forced to bring children to appointments with their solicitor.

Notes

8 This report is being published at a time of great change within the NHS. The 2012 Health and Social Care Act, which came into effect in April 2013 puts clinicians at the centre of commissioning care (Department of Health, 2012). The newly formed NHS Commissioning Board has taken on the function of Primary Care Trusts and will run primary care services, such as GP practices. It is yet to be seen what impact these changes will have on refugee women's experiences of primary health care services. In the move towards more localised decision-making regarding the commissioning of primary health care services the author hopes that GP services will be more able to respond to the needs of their communities, particularly in areas with high refugee populations.

Discussion and recommendations

© Neal Sanche